ONE STOP

The One Stop Series

Series editor: David Martin, FCIS, FIPD, FCB
                Buddenbrook Consultancy

A series of practical, user-friendly yet authoritative titles designed to provide a one stop guide to key topics in business administration.

Other books in the series to date include:

David Martin	*One Stop Company Secretary*, second edition
David Martin	*One Stop Personnel,* second edition
Jeremy Stranks	*One Stop Health and Safety*
John Wyborn	*One Stop Contracts*
David Martin	*One Stop Property*
Harris Rosenberg	*One Stop Finance*
Robert Leach	*One Stop Payroll*
David Martin/ John Wyborn	*One Stop Negotiation*
David Martin	*One Stop Communication*
Karen Huntingford	*One Stop Insurance*
David Martin	*One Stop Customer Care*
Patrick Forsyth	*One Stop Marketing*

ONE STOP
Leadership

JEREMY KOURDI

ICSA Publishing

Published by ICSA Publishing Limited
16 Park Crescent
London W1N 4AH

© ICSA Publishing Ltd 1999

All rights reserved. No part of this publication may be reproduced, stored in a retrieval system, or transmitted, in any form, or by any means, electronic, mechanical, photocopying, recording or otherwise, without prior permission, in writing, from the publisher.

Typeset in 10/12.5 pt Meridien with Frutiger Light
by Fakenham Photosetting Ltd, Fakenham, Norfolk

Printed and bound in Great Britain
by TJ International Ltd, Padstow, Cornwall

British Library Cataloguing in Publication Data

A catalogue record for this book is available from the British Library

ISBN: 1-860720-85-4

Contents

Acknowledgements	vi	Leading for the first time	103
Preface	vii	Leading other leaders	107
Appraisals	1	Managing finance and profitability	111
Benchmarking and managing competitiveness	9	Mentoring and coaching	125
Business ethics	17	Motivation and empowerment	135
Change management	27	Negotiating skills	141
Communications skills	31	Problem-solving	155
Creativity and innovation	39	Project management	161
Decision-making	45	Staff planning and interviewing	171
Delegating effectively	53	Strategic planning	179
Developing yourself and your staff	63	Stress management	185
Financial leadership and building shareholder value	71	Team-building and developing high-performing teams	191
Handling conflict	77	Time management	203
Knowledge management	83	Total quality management (TQM) and business process re-engineering (BPR)	209
Leadership skills	87	Vision and transformation	217
Leadership styles and organisational culture	93		

Acknowledgements

Managing authors successfully is always a difficult and skilful task, and supporting publishers who become authors is even harder. This task has been accomplished with great skill by David Martin, *One Stop* series editor and himself one of the UK's most successful business writers, and Clare Grist Taylor at the ICSA.

In writing this book I have tried to convey some of the skills and techniques acquired during my career, and I have been truly fortunate to have worked with a number of excellent leaders too numerous to mention here. These people understand that success is entirely about effective leadership and getting the best from people, and that to achieve this requires diligence and (particularly when working with me) a good sense of humour.

Finally, my family, Julie, Thomas and Louise Kourdi, have provided an indispensable source of help, support and sustenance. This book is dedicated to them.

Preface

This book is designed to provide a ready source of information and guidance for leaders at all levels. For ease of use and reference it has been necessary to split the topic of leadership into clearly defined sections, although in reality many of the topics interrelate and impact on each other. For example, TEAM-BUILDING, MOTIVATION, MENTORING and LEADERSHIP STYLES are all closely related, and can be read together as well as separately.

Many of the key processes for effective leadership share stages in an ongoing cycle: consider, plan, communicate, implement, monitor and evaluate, consider . . . This approach is frequently used in the topics covered in this book and it is a touchstone for successful leadership.

It is also important to emphasise that leadership is not simply exercised in a commercial business environment – although that is probably the biggest single area of activity where leaders are to be found – but in virtually every area of life. This ranges from the cradle to the grave, and whilst this book covers the application of leadership in business, it is written to provide information and guidance for leaders in *any* sphere of activity, including public service, charitable work, the military, education, science and others.

Finally, this book is intended as a guide to stimulate and support effective leadership: in a time of constant, far-reaching change, the need for industry and commerce to be led by effective leaders is greater than ever.

Jeremy Kourdi

Appraisals

Introduction

Appraisals are widely used, both formally and informally, to help leaders encourage people to become more effective in their work. In fact, there are four general reasons for appraisals:

1. To *agree* performance-related targets.
2. To review overall *performance* across a period of time and *reward* individuals.
3. To focus on the *development needs* of individuals so that they can achieve their goals more effectively.
4. To *communicate* and provide information and feedback.

Agreeing targets can be seen as the key to effective appraisals and should be actively 'sold' as the major benefit. This helps to ensure that the process is positive and forward-looking, and does not provide a less than satisfactory opportunity to apportion blame.

An effective appraisal system helps leaders to learn more about their team members, their problems and needs, where the challenges and opportunities lie, and how their aspirations are being fulfilled by their job. (This in turn can help the leader to motivate their team.) In addition, regular, structured appraisals can be an enormously powerful tool for improving sustained individual performance and productivity.

The benefits of appraisals

There are several advantages that result from appraisal schemes.

The *organisation* benefits from:

- Regular, comparable, standard information about its personnel.
- The opportunity to tailor and focus development activities for individuals based on appraisal information (this is also a major advantage for the leader).

- An accurate plan of its human resource needs – from staffing levels to training and development requirements.

The *leader* benefits from:

- The opportunity to build trust, provide advice and feedback, and motivate and develop an improved relationship with their team members.
- Improved understanding of staff development needs – their strengths and weaknesses.

Individuals benefit from:

- An objective assessment of their job performance, including their strengths and weaknesses.
- Considering and planning their development needs, including future training.
- A greater understanding of the needs of the job and their manager, and an improved relationship with their manager.

Techniques for ensuring effective appraisals

Prepare for the appraisal (sometimes also known as the role review)

The leader and the team member both need to prepare for an appraisal to succeed. The leader's preparation can include:

- Reviewing the team member's record of performance, projects, workload, problem areas, strengths, weaknesses and potential development opportunities.
- Checking the arrangements for the appraisal, including the room, timing and the team member's expectations.

Maintain an open, positive atmosphere for the appraisal

Right from the start the leader should take a welcoming, frank and positive approach to the meeting. The leader should:

- *Reach agreement with the team member about the purpose and focus of the review,* including any ground-rules (e.g. emphasising confidentiality) that may be necessary.
- *Provide the team member with the opportunity to comment* with their views and participate in the discussion. It should be a two-way process!
- *Avoid being patronising and insincere* – honesty and openness work best.

- *Emphasise success*, as success can be built upon. Problem areas should be faced and dealt with clearly.
- *Provide direction, challenge the team member on specific issues and clearly explain their point of view.* This will avoid problems and frustrations later, but may need to be handled sensitively to maintain commitment.

Review performance and reach agreement

This is central to the appraisal process and requires that the leader:

- is prepared, with a clear view of what the best outcome for the discussion would be;
- is constructive and honest;
- keeps comments specific and focused, and can provide examples;
- avoids unpleasant surprises for the team member that will damage the rapport and reduce (or end) the effectiveness of the meeting;
- promotes a genuine discussion;
- sets clear targets and agrees these with the individual. Targets should ideally be specific, attainable, relevant and time-related;
- confirms agreement, perhaps by summarising during the discussion and/or at the end (depending on complexity);
- addresses the learning and development needs of the individual;
- considers the issue of pay and benefits: What would be the best response if the team member asks for a raise? (A common event that is often saved for appraisals!);
- is prepared to provide additional help and support, and follows through with any commitments.

Giving feedback and dealing with reactions

Preparation is vital for an effective appraisal and includes understanding what needs to be said and discussed, *as well as the team member's likely response*. Whilst most people will accept the leader's assessment and views, probably with input and comments of their own, there may be times when more challenging reactions occur. Table 1 lists potential reactions and suggested responses.

Consider reward systems

The team member will be concerned with their future and current prospects; the leader therefore needs to review and monitor the system of pay and rewards to ensure that the team member is motivated and feels

ONE STOP LEADERSHIP

Reaction	Solution
The team member firmly disagrees	If the disagreement is over a point of fact, then the best approach is to put the issue to one side, check the facts and come back to the individual later. It may be that you have made a mistake and if so this should be admitted. If the person disagrees with your views or approach, then the best tack is to discover why they feel that way, what are their concerns and can they be overcome? This discussion is essential for the appraisal process to work and provide benefit.
The team member becomes emotional	Stay calm, listen and absorb the emotional outburst; if feasible, allow the person time to calm down and then continue. If this is not practical then end the meeting and agree to resume at another time. Remember that the outburst may be a tactic intended to manipulate the leader or avoid an outcome that the individual does not like. Stay calm at all times but be firm and clear if you think that this might be the case.
The team member is too passive, disinterested or refuses to take the appraisal seriously	Consider forcing the team member to summarise your points and criticisms and give their own comments on them. If this does not draw them into the appraisal then get tougher with a question such as 'Why are you not taking this seriously?' or 'What do you think will happen if this continues?' Finally, it helps in extreme cases to wield a big stick, e.g. 'Do you realise that unless you focus on these issues . . .'
The team member blames someone (or something) else for causing their problems	This may, of course, be justified and the leader should certainly consider this first. However, blame-shifting often occurs when people receive negative feedback. The solution usually lies in fully exploring the problem and understanding the basic points.

Reaction	Solution
The team member is uncommunicative or behaves out of character	Often this is caused by a lingering fear, preoccupation or concern that the person has, or misgivings about the appraisal process. The solution is to reassure them about the appraisal and encourage their response in a particular area. If this still fails then ask if they are concerned about something and explore any issues or concerns.

Table 1 Techniques for dealing with negative reactions

valued. Reward systems and benefits to consider for staff include: merit pay awards; individual or team performance-related bonuses; profit-sharing; holidays; insurance benefits (e.g. private health care); pensions; share schemes.

Case study: *The dangers of process-driven appraisals*

A relatively new employee had her first ever appraisal; she was understandably anxious about how it would go, and this anxiety was fuelled by a lengthy form that had to be completed and brought to the appraisal interview. However, instead of delivering a hostile inquisition the manager focused exclusively on the needs of the form and the process, rather than using it as a tool to appraise the employee's performance. As the appraisal progressed the manager became both relieved to be completing the form, and dismissive or defensive when the employee pressed for any meaningful feedback. The result was a process completed and boxes ticked, but at the expense of the employee losing interest, ownership and respect.

The message seems clear: it is often easy to lose sight of the *purpose* of the appraisal, i.e. what is being said and how performance is being developed, when there is too great an emphasis on documentation and other appraisal tools.

Avoiding common problems

Preparation by both the team member and the leader will help to pre-empt any difficulties. Encouraging team members to participate actively in the discussion should help to overcome any problems. This might involve the team member being asked to comment on their performance, strengths, weaknesses and areas for further development.

Be aware of common problem areas. These may include:

- *Too much emphasis on the appraisal process and documentation* – it is there for your benefit, not the other way around! There is also a danger that the leader will stick too rigidly to the appraisal structure. Essentially the process needs to provide a genuine exploration of needs, issues and problems, and this may require a fluid, flexible style (e.g. asking open questions, and exploring points as they arise).
- *Dwelling too much on the past* – this should not really account for more than 50 per cent of the discussion; future activities, priorities, development needs and objectives should also be discussed.
- *Being too directive, highly critical or being **perceived** as being critical* – in order to work, the appraisal needs to be a dynamic, positive discussion, not a witch-hunt or a chance to heap blame and ignominy on someone. (If this needs to be done, it should follow the offending action and not be stored up for the appraisal!)
- *Giving comments and feedback poorly* – this can include being unclear about the points that need to be made or 'beating about the bush' rather than being honest and open with your comments.
- *Not understanding what the team member has done (or failed to do)* – to prevent this the leader should prepare and this can include discretely getting comments from colleagues.

Summary: *Managing successful appraisals*

Ensure that:

- The appraisal process has clearly identifiable outcomes and that these are agreed and communicated to all involved.
- The appraisal process is tailored to the needs of your specific organisation; large, detailed and involved schemes are unlikely to work well in small organisations and may lead to misunderstandings and ill-will.

- People are consulted when deciding how they will be rewarded.
- You listen to what is being said and ensure that your points are prepared and well communicated.
- You consider the individual's work and performance in the context of the whole team or organisation.
- Constructive criticism is provided.

Avoid:

- Facing a problem or discussing a difficult issue if it is unnecessary.
- Dwelling on what went wrong and what problems or difficulties people may have; try to understand these points quickly and then focus on *why* it happened and what needs to be done to resolve the situation in the future.
- Relying on the comments of others – always appraise people based on your own experience of their work.

Further information

Successful Appraisals in a Week
D. Kamp, Hodder Headline, 1994

Appraising Your Staff
P. Moon, Kogan Page, 1993

Performance Appraisals
M. Fisher, Kogan Page, 1995

Appraisal: Routes to improved performance
C. Fletcher, Institute of Personnel and Development, 1993

360 Degree Appraisal (Managing Best Practice)
Industrial Society, 1995

One Stop Personnel
D. Martin, ICSA Publishing, second edition 1999

Benchmarking and managing competitiveness

Introduction

Benchmarking is the ongoing process of measuring all aspects of performance against the best in the field and then learning from those practices to improve success. Benchmarking usually works best when an organisation is concerned with total quality management (TQM). It is a technique that continues to gain in popularity as it is viewed as an important means of building competitiveness.

Benchmarking involves the organisation in:

- continuously looking at itself and analysing its performance and internal processes;
- continuously planning and implementing improvements;
- maintaining an open, positive and supportive style of leadership and organisation structure which promotes this approach.

Why benchmarking is increasingly supported by organisations

1. It clearly focuses organisations on improving their performance *relative to their competitors.*
2. It promotes continuous improvement.
3. It fosters greater process efficiency and effectiveness.
4. It provides an external perspective, which can counterbalance an emphasis on internal procedures.

Why benchmarking is increasingly favoured by leaders

1. It helps to solve specific problems.
2. It helps individuals to avoid making the mistakes of others.
3. It helps to identify areas for improvement.
4. It is useful in establishing realistic, relevant and valuable goals and objectives.
5. It helps people to become the best.
6. It constantly challenges and stretches people's performance.

Types of benchmarking

There are generally recognised to be four types of benchmarking:

1. *Internal* – where parts of the same organisation are compared (e.g. General Motors manufacturing operations in the USA compared with those in the UK).
2. *Competitive* – where performance against direct competitors is, *as far as possible,* assessed.
3. *Functional* – this involves comparisons with other organisations that carry out one or more of the same functional activities (e.g. warehousing).
4. *Generic* – this is used for comparisons across business functions or industries. For example, payment terms in the printing industry compared to advertising.

Method of benchmarking	Key features	Advantages	Disadvantages
INTERNAL	Comparison with other parts of the same organisation. This can include other companies within the same group and also works internationally.	• Information is readily available and usable. • Results can be spread across the organisation.	• Unlikely to 'break the mould' or yield world-class improvements.
COMPETITIVE	Information relating to the standards of direct competitors is assessed, and used as a source of improvement.	• Directly targets competitor advantages. • Yields valuable insights.	• It can be very difficult to obtain the necessary information. • Organisations can look as if they are copying or trailing in the wake of their competitors.
FUNCTIONAL	Organisations compare their functional activities with those of other	• Useful as a means for evaluating costs and whether to outsource. • Confidentiality is	• Cultural factors – i.e. adapting new processes from outside a business or

Method of benchmarking	Key features	Advantages	Disadvantages
	non-competitive organisations.	not a problem – in fact, the opposite is true: many companies are willing to discuss performance to sell their services.	industry – can cause problems.
GENERIC	This compares business processes which go *across* different functions and industries.	• Typically these generate the most innovative breakthroughs and process improvements.	• Whilst the gains can be high, the difficulties in adapting and introducing radically new concepts can be challenging.

Table 2 Methods of benchmarking

European Business Excellence Model and the Baldridge Quality Award

Many organisations prefer to measure aspects of their performance against an artificial, 'idealised' standard such as those provided in the USA, Europe and Japan. The advantages are that it is easier: the research phase is largely eliminated and what matters is measuring up to the standards, and planning and implementing improvements, not the other tasks of measurement and assessment; the disadvantage is that these programmes can be rather non-specific, However, evidence suggests that they can be of considerable value for most organisations.

Techniques for implementing benchmarking in your organisation

Ensure senior management commitment

As with any major, wide-ranging performance improvement project there needs to be commitment from the top of the organisation. This will ensure that:

- The initiative is taken seriously and receives the necessary momentum.
- The right level of resource – particularly in terms of time, money and

expertise – is available. Benchmarking can be very resource-intensive and time-consuming, but if completed successfully it can deliver impressive and worthwhile results. (The greatest threat to benchmarking is often short-termism as the effects of different processes, their strengths and weaknesses, need to be assessed over time. They then need to be adapted to, and implemented, in the new organisation.)

- Organisational structures are changed so that benchmarking becomes an established, accepted part of the business.
- Information is available to those that need it.
- Individuals have the authority to act, and once approved can implement the results of the benchmarking process.

Develop a benchmarking team

The people that need to be directly involved in the benchmarking process are:

- *The process champion* – the manager responsible for co-ordinating the process, generating enthusiasm for the challenges of continuous improvement and driving forward the initiative.
- *The process owners* – undoubtedly the most important people involved in the initiative are the process owners: people whose processes are being benchmarked and who, as a result of the initiative, will later be expected to make effective changes. Not only do their hearts and minds need to be in the project, their knowledge and expertise are also fundamentally important.
- *Researchers/analysts/initiators* – this group needs to include people that can research and objectively analyse the organisation's processes, strengths and weaknesses. They need to be able to:
  - identify instances of best (or better) practice; and
  - devise practical ways of implementing best practice, with the support of the process owners and facilitators.
- *Facilitators/consultants/trainers* – functional specialists that can deliver the necessary training and help to implement the process improvements.

Understand and improve the organisation's internal processes – use critical success factors

One of the earliest stages in the benchmarking process *is for the organisation to understand its own internal processes*. This means knowing:

- what the *critical success factors* (i.e. the key determinants of success or failure) within the organisation are;
- how they affect success or failure;

- how they can be measured;
- how they can be improved.

Table 3 provides a framework for the leader to review and implement changes to critical success factors:

Critical success factor	What is the current level of performance?	What is a realistic target?	Action plan for improvements	Target date	Who is responsible?
1					
2					
3					
4					
5					

Table 3 Assessing critical success factors

The key questions when using critical success factors to improve performance are:

- What factors determine the success of your organisation?
- What are the core business processes in your organisation?
- Have you analysed your core business processes?
- Do you know (is there a list of) all the stages for each business process, including inputs, outputs and process owners?
- How can you measure the success (or quality) of each process?
- Have you set targets for each process?
- Are these measurable, realistic and time-specific?
- How will you achieve these targets?

Research and analyse data and ideas

Benchmarking requires research into business processes in order to understand:

1. how competitors achieve better performance in certain areas; and
2. how to improve performance generally (not necessarily using the experiences of competitors).

The methods that are chosen depend on the type of benchmarking (i.e. internal, competitive, functional or generic) that is being followed. Information can be acquired from:

- trade journals, conferences, seminars, libraries, books, periodicals
- the Internet
- trade associations

- customers
- suppliers
- business schools and research institutes
- government agencies
- other non-competitive organisations wishing to benchmark aspects of their business
- networking
- industry visits and site surveys
- questionnaires and interviews
- market research companies
- employees.

Researching, collating and storing data are fundamental to the task of benchmarking. Anyone following such an initiative needs to possess these skills or have ready access to them. Most initiatives use databases to store information and help with analysis, although there are several points to note:

- Ensure compliance with the current data protection legislation.
- Try to collect data that are directly comparable with your own – it makes the task of interpreting and applying the data much easier, especially seeing where the gaps in performance lie.
- Consider communicating the information that is held widely, so that people can easily understand the benefits of the benchmarking programme.

Case study: *Benchmarking for competitive advantage*

There are a number of spectacular examples of organisations that have benchmarked their business against every aspect of their competitors' operations, and then implemented changes that have either turned around a declining business or ensured that a new product launch is successful. Benchmarking can often be most effective when it combines information from other businesses with a high degree of innovation and inventiveness.

For example, it is often argued that Virgin Atlantic set a new standard for transatlantic air travel by studying their competitors and identifying the market opportunity they could best exploit, and then

> aggressively realising this opportunity. At a time when air prices were rising and bookings falling they launched a lower priced (and lower cost) service, against the prevailing wisdom in the industry. They then capitalised on this with a number of popular measures that gained them attention and complemented their approach: everything from ice creams to refresh long-distance travellers to courier services to and from airports.
>
> Similarly, the popular and successful Novotel chain of hotels derived in large part from a study of the hotel industry in France, where – in essence – there were expensive, high-quality hotels, and inexpensive, low-standard hotels. This benchmarking of the industry was cross-referenced with customer requirements, and the concept of a cheap hotel with certain 'quality' features (e.g. en suite facilities, satellite TV, telephones) as standard resulted.
>
> What may seem glaringly obvious now can often only become apparent after a practical benchmarking exercise that reveals exactly what is done and how – as well as what is *not* done.

Act decisively to implement initiatives

This is the key stage of the whole process for the leader; it is the purpose of benchmarking and is the part of the programme that delivers success or failure. To support the process and minimise the risks of failure the leader should:

- Review the findings of the benchmarking programme, ideally involving relevant process owners, highlighting and trying to resolve any areas of uncertainty.
- Discuss with others the findings and the best response: how to change internal processes and critical success factors successfully.
- Prepare the business case, including timing, cost and resource issues, targets and expected benefits.
- Communicate the new approach.
- Train and prepare people so that the new targets can be achieved.
- Direct and motivate so that the necessary changes are implemented.

The final stage of this process is one of constant monitoring and evaluation, to review progress and ensure continued success.

> **Summary:** *Effective benchmarking*
>
> Effective benchmarking therefore requires:
>
> - Information to be as accurate, reliable and comprehensive as possible.
> - The ability to understand and audit the organisation's own internal procedures.
> - A dynamic, flexible approach that can adapt to changes in external circumstances.
> - Targets to be *realistic and worthwhile*. This means ensuring that they are attainable, but also based on industry standards – if this is difficult to achieve immediately, then it could be targeted as a strategic goal for the organisation
> - Integration with the organisation's strategic and operational plans.

Further information

Benchmarking for Competitive Advantage
Bendell, Kelly and Boulter,
FT/Pitman, 1993

The Benchmarking Workout
Bendell, Kelly and Boulter,
FT/Pitman, 1996

Competitive Strategy: techniques for analysing industry and competitors
M. Porter, The Free Press, 1980

Competitive Advantage – Creating and sustaining superior performance
M. Porter, The Free Press, 1985

Business ethics

Introduction

The issue of ethics in business management is wide-ranging, and while it has always been in the background it has now achieved a level of significance that few people – let alone leaders – can afford to ignore. The rise in prominence of business ethics has been caused in part by a number of shattering corporate scandals around the world – the Lockheed scandal in the USA during the 1970s, the collapse of the bank BCCI and the awarding of the Olympic Games by the International Olympic Committee to certain cities, being some of the most notable examples of the recent era.

Ethics remain important in business because of their impact on business: more than ever before organisations are under pressure from governments, customers, employees and others to adopt a more ethical stance. Many companies have now embraced ethics and social responsibility, using them for differentiation and to gain competitive advantage.

Some of the issues affected by business ethics include:

- investment trusts
- pension rights
- employment issues such as discrimination and harassment
- social cause marketing
- environmentalism
- privacy
- advertising and marketing
- corruption.

Research into business ethics

A good deal of research into business ethics has been undertaken in the UK and USA. The key findings relating to the UK showed:

How common are ethical codes?

- 47 per cent of organisations have codes of ethics; 48 per cent of organ-

isations do not, and 5 per cent of managerial respondents were unsure whether their organisation did or not.
- 53 per cent of organisations with 500 or more employees have codes, rising to 81 per cent of those with over 50,000 employees. Codes are more common in large organisations, the public sector, financial services and utilities.

Do leaders favour professional ethical codes?

Overwhelmingly, 74 per cent agree that codes are a constructive measure.

Do you adopt an ethical approach to management?

- 96 per cent of respondents believe that as managers they should give ethical leadership.
- 82 per cent of managers use their own moral values to decide on ethical issues.
- Surprisingly, 30 per cent of respondents identify senior management as the main obstacle to ethical management in their organisation.

Which ethical matters are of the greatest concern to leaders?

Respondents cited the following main issues:

- environmental matters
- public morals
- the quality of their product or service
- professional performance relating to internally set standards of conduct.

Types of unethical behaviour

The following behaviours were viewed as ethical issues within organisations:

Employment issues

- Knowingly providing poor quality goods
- Using the organisation's assets and equipment for personal use
- Inaccurate accounting
- Giving and receiving excessive gifts or hospitality
- Overcharging customers/clients
- Delaying settling debts
- Large salaries and above-average percentage pay rises for top executives
- Excessive (unjustifiable) expense account claims
- Theft
- Discrimination (most commonly sex and race, but also religious, disability and age)
- Unsafe working conditions

External relationships

- Bribery to win contracts
- Causing environmental damage
- Large financial donations to political parties
- Industrial espionage
- Commercial and financial (i.e. investment) links with repressive regimes
- Spreading disinformation about individuals and competitors
- Misrepresenting products and services in advertising
- Marketing which exploits the 'weak' in society
- Withholding information from shareholder
- Drug and alcohol abuse at work
- Poor handling of redundancies
- Breaching confidentiality
- Personal harassment.

(Sources: *Institute of Management; Institute of Personnel and Development; American Management Association*)

Ethical issues

The terms 'ethics' and 'ethical behaviour' are notoriously difficult to define in relation to business; however, some of the following issues affect the way that leaders run their organisations.

Accepting gifts and benefits

Accepting gifts is an inescapable part of business in certain cultures and parts of the world. In most instances it is entirely proper and sincerely meant; however, there are several fundamental questions to be considered before accepting gifts or entertainment:

1. What is the motive behind the present?
2. How could your influence be given in return for favours?
3. How would it appear to others? (*Everyone* else.)
4. Is it reasonable?
5. Is it justifiable?
6. Will there be any ongoing repercussions of accepting the gift?

Gifts and bribery may not always be the start of the process, but can often be the result of extortion. For example, suppliers may provide customers with lavish gifts, payments or favours because they know that if they do not, they will lose that customer. Whilst still wrong, it should, perhaps, influence how it is viewed and the severity of action taken.

Employment and discrimination

Everyone has different expectations, standards and levels of tolerance. Many areas – an increasing number – are now covered by employment legislation as well as other agreements (e.g. with unions); however, there is a vast area of expectation that has to be covered by the organisation observing ethical values and norms. Best practice in this area means:

- Never discriminating against anyone. When people are 'decided against' then it must be purely for job-related reasons.
- Recognising and ending different types of discrimination, including:
  - *Individual discrimination*, which occurs when members of the organisation are prejudiced;
  - *Structural discrimination*, when prejudice is a part of the system, for example affecting job or promotion conditions;
  - *Occupational discrimination*, when it is commonly assumed that some groups are incapable of performing certain tasks.
- Respecting people, their privacy and rights. The divide between work and home is a notoriously difficult one, and a general rule is to avoid it and always to treat information confidentially. Nevertheless, the employer certainly has the right to know what factors may be adversely affecting performance, and this is generally accepted.

Increasingly, firms are implementing 'family-friendly' policies such as flexitime working, crèche facilities, maternity and paternity leave, etc., in order to attract and retain key staff. This brings with it significant new responsibilities for the employer and also changes the culture of the organisation. Many of these issues are included in the European Commission's Social Chapter and may affect all businesses as a matter of course (for further information see *One Stop Personnel* by David Martin).

Marketing and selling

Satisfying customer needs should ensure that there is a positive ethical aspect to advertising and marketing; however, this is occasionally hampered by the fact that the customer is vulnerable in certain areas if left uninformed. There is much in the way of legislation and codes of conduct that is designed to protect consumers, but they can still remain vulnerable to issues such as:

- pricing (including predatory pricing techniques);
- targeting naive members of society (e.g. children);
- being clear and unequivocal about product contents, ingredients, production techniques (where there are concerns) and origins;

- ensuring safety and displaying warnings – particularly for items such as electrical appliances, tamper-proof and child-proof packaging.

Handling ethical issues

Fair trading and corporate social responsibility have become important to many organisations, and the issue of ethics has been used by many organisations to improve the ways that they do business: finding better solutions to problems, exploiting opportunities and achieving success. Many business writers and researchers have highlighted the fact that adopting an ethical approach to business does not necessarily mean adopting an *altruistic* approach. Leaders considering how to develop an ethical awareness and perspective within their organisation might contemplate:

- *Positive discrimination (favouring previously disadvantaged groups)* – this can be a popular remedy to certain ethical problems, although the disadvantages include the risk of creating new victims, lowering morale and motivation, and having a disproportionate effect on the problem.
- *Affirmative action (planning and executing deliberate measures to remove structural imbalances)* – tends to be more popular and successful than positive discrimination, especially in the areas of recruitment, interviewing and training.
- *Codes of ethics (these are a public commitment to ethical business, contained in a published code of operating principles)* – the greatest difficulties that organisations and leaders face in this area are: first, translating well-intentioned principles into effective guidelines, and then putting them into practice. Second, monitoring, policing and enforcing ethical standards of behaviour within organisations. However, codes of ethics can be effective ways of introducing and reinforcing ethical standards, and are increasingly popular.

Case study: *The Body Shop*

The Body Shop started trading in the mid-1970s providing environmentally-friendly toiletries and cosmetics. It soon developed into a massively popular UK retailer, and its distinctiveness was due in large part to the high-profile ethical stance of the business and its founders, Anita and Gordon Roddick. This ethical stance has in many ways defined the business, and the Body Shop uses its environmental policies (such as providing reusable packaging; campaigning against animal testing, and promoting fair trade with the third

> world) as a source of competitive advantage and publicity. At times this has caused a cynical backlash, but the uncompromising, ethical approach has remained and sustained the business. The approach encompasses most areas including purchasing, development, marketing and publicity, training and recruitment. Today the Body Shop remains a clear and striking example of the power of ethics in business.

Codes of ethics

The difficulty with ethical issues in business is that if the leader or organisation does nothing in this area, then they leave themselves open to unethical acts and all the problems that could ensue. But if they do act they are frequently criticised for 'jumping on the band wagon', cynically using the issue of ethics as a cheap publicity stunt. Fortunately, as ethical behaviour becomes more widespread and the issue continues to gain acceptance, there is a growing belief that organisations can only succeed if they and their leaders embrace an ethical stance.

Codes of ethics can address both of these issues, and can be defined as:

> ... *guidelines to a set of moral principles or values, used by organisations to steer the conduct both of the organisation itself and its employees, in all their business activities, both internal and in relation to the outside world.*
>
> (Institute of Management)

Benefits of codes of ethics

- They promote a culture of excellence by clearly showing the commitment of the organisation to ethical standards of behaviour. This can help to provide clear direction and motivation.
- Codes provide explicit guidance to new and existing managers and employees, so that they know what is expected of them and also attain a sense of common identity.
- They enhance the organisation's reputation, inspiring public confidence and demonstrating to their customers and suppliers the standards that are expected.

Potential pitfalls of ethical codes

- The code can cause severe cynicism and demotivation if it is not effectively supported by leaders and implemented.
- Codes that are poorly drafted can be equivocal, open to interpretation

and confusing, particularly in large, multi-site organisations. This in turn undermines their value and effectiveness.
- The code can raise expectations both inside and outside the organisation, and will require time and commitment from the organisation's leader to implement.
- Codes can be devised too late. This in turn often leads to cynicism and difficulty in implementing them effectively.

Developing a code of ethics

1. *Ensure top management commitment* – the leaders of the organisation need to support the code fully in how they act as well as in what they say, and they need to promote it actively to their employees, explaining what it is and why it matters.

> **Case study:** *The European Commission*
>
> A high-profile example of the importance of codes of ethics came in March 1999, when all twenty European Commissioners resigned following publication of a highly critical report into cases of fraud, mismanagement and nepotism within the Commission. Needless to say, this was a hugely complex affair riven with politics and largely the outcome of the entrenched working practices of the Commission, established over many years. Yet in many ways it was foreseeable and preventable.
>
> The European Commission had been perceived as being inefficient and open to abuse for years, perhaps decades. With its critics lining up and popular support steadily ebbing away, leaders now acknowledge that effective action should have been taken to ensure that its members followed acceptable standards of behaviour. The crisis – when it hit – was almost inevitable, and whatever the substance of the actual charges they probably matter less than the damage done to the reputation of the Commission. It now seems likely that a code of ethics or standards will, belatedly, be implemented along the lines of that adopted in recent years for British parliamentarians. However, this episode highlights the fact that an organisation not only needs to adopt ethical standards of behaviour, but it often *needs to be seen to do so* as well.

2. *Define the scope and purpose of the code* – the *scope* of the code needs to be understood: for example whether it will affect employees, or others with a stake in the organisation such as suppliers and non-executive directors. The *purpose* of the code also needs to be clear: what areas and types of issue is it primarily concerned with?
3. *Understand the likely effects of the code and how practical it will be to implement.* The likely *effects* of the code need to be assessed: these include tangible aspects such as changing suppliers, advertising or investments; or intangibles such as shifting the culture of the organisation and encountering the problems of whistle blowing.
4. *Develop a code that reflects a consensus within the organisation* – existing documents and policies, such as mission statements or staff handbooks, should be evaluated and allowed to influence the code, or else revised to meet the new requirements. External organisations – other similar organisations or professional and regulatory bodies – can also provide guidelines.
5. *Ensure that the code of ethics is grounded in reality i.e. that it is understandable, consistent and workable* – the code should reflect the culture of the organisation and what can be achieved in practice. If it is too divorced from reality, it will be ignored. If it is too ineffectual, it will similarly be disregarded.
6. *Build broad support and ownership for the code of ethics* – this could involve appointing a small, representative group advising on the development of the code. It may also be worth including comments from anyone within the organisation who has something valuable to offer, at any level. Circulate the draft widely and consider *all* responses. Quite apart from helping to develop the code it will also reinforce awareness and begin the process of implementation.
7. *Consider including in the code:*

    - an *introduction* outlining the code's purpose and the expectations for its use;
    - operating principles and *guidance on behaviour*, ideally with examples;
    - *guidance on handling relations* with groups such as employees, suppliers, shareholders and others;
    - a formal *operating mechanism* to implement the code and handle any questions, complaints or concerns. This may include disciplinary or investigation procedures.

8. *Circulate the code widely and decide how it should be implemented* – it is often best to appoint one person who will champion the code, explaining its purpose and what it is expected to achieve. The code should also be incorporated into routine procedures such as staff induction and training, and it should be kept up to date.

9. *Monitor the code's relevance and effectiveness – and update it when necessary.* Codes of ethics should not be allowed to become outdated; someone needs to have responsibility for ensuring that it is reviewed and updated, and properly implemented.

Summary:	*Implementing a code of ethics*

The range of ethical issues in business at times appears boundless. Almost any decision can be given an ethical slant, and because of this the future for business ethics as a separate business topic is not good. This is not because it is unimportant – on the contrary, ethics in business are vital and long overdue in coming – it is because ethics are often subject to flagrant and frequent misuse: almost any action can be defended by giving it an ethical slant. It is therefore prudent to treat with caution anyone using ethics as a justification for action, while it is equally important to develop one's own ethical sense of what is right and reasonable, and what is wrong, and to use that as a guiding framework for action.

Key steps when implementing a code of ethics. You should:

1. *Ensure that it is integrated into the business* – a strategy needs to be developed for integrating the code into the routine running of the business.
2. *Obtain endorsement* – ensure that the code is clearly supported and promoted by the chief executive.
3. *Communicate and distribute the code* – ensure that a copy of the code is given to all employees, as well as to all new employees. The code should also be made available to business contacts (such as suppliers and customers). Finally, ensure that it is distributed across the organisation including, for example, overseas subsidiaries.
4. *Provide guidance* – the code should include a section on how employees should act when faced with a potential breach of the code of ethics. This could also include advice on what to do when making an ethical decision, and how to seek further advice.

5. *Ensure that the code is active and adhered to* – this can be achieved through effective promotion of the code, explaining what it is and why it matters. Allowing people to respond to the code and even to assist in its development will help to make it realistic, comprehensive and workable. Finally, a formal procedure for checking understanding of the code is valuable in highlighting its importance (e.g. include the code with employees' contracts of employment, which they must sign, and link it with formal disciplinary procedures).
6. *Regularly review and monitor the code* – this helps to ensure that it is kept up to date.
7. *Integrate the code into training practices* – where possible include the appropriate aspects of the code in staff training. Training in marketing, purchasing or negotiating, for example, could benefit from an ethical perspective, as could many aspects of managing and leading people.

In-depth case studies and codes of ethics are available on the Internet as well as from the following organisations:

- Institute of Business Ethics, 12 Palace Street, London SW1E 5JA. Tel. 0171 931 0495
- Institute of Management, Management House, Cottingham Road, Corby, Northants NN17 1TT. Tel. 01536 204222

Further information

Company Use of Codes of Business Conduct
Martin Le Jeune and Simon Webley, Institute of Business Ethics, 1998

An Introduction to Business Ethics
G. Chrysiddes and J. Kaler, Chapman and Hall, 1993

Handbook of Good Business Practice
W. Manley, Routledge, 1992

The Manager as a Professional
Sheila Evers, Institute of Management, 1993

One Stop Personnel
D. Martin, ICSA, second edition 1999

Change management

> **Introduction**
>
> It is often said that the only constant in business is change. The task of initiating, directing and controlling that change for the greatest benefit falls to the leader. There are several valuable techniques that will contribute to successful change. These are applicable in a wide range of scenarios, including:
>
> - mergers and acquisitions
> - corporate reorganisations
> - major new projects
> - performance improvement initiatives.

Checklist – the eight-stage process of creating major change

This process was first outlined by John Kotter in his best-selling work *Leading Change*, which clearly describes what the leader needs to do to ensure that beneficial change is achieved.

1. Establishing a sense of urgency

The leader should initiate – or take control of – the process by emphasising the need for change. The more urgent and pressing the need, the more likely it is that people's attention and commitment will be focused. Usually the leader's role is to stay positive and build on success. However, at this point it helps to emphasise *failure*: what might go wrong, how, when and what the consequences could be.

- For a commercial operation this can include examining market pressures and competitive realities.
- For all types of organisation it involves identifying and discussing crises or potential crises.
- The leader can also emphasise positive elements, perhaps highlighting potential windows of opportunity that require swift and effective change.

2. Creating the guiding coalition

The guiding coalition needs to understand the purpose of the change process: what it is intended to achieve. This group should be united, co-ordinated and carry significant authority and respect within the organisation. It needs to have the power to make things happen, fundamentally changing systems and procedures where necessary, but it also needs the respect of people so that it can lead them along too.

3. Developing a vision and strategy

The leader and the guiding coalition need to create a simple, powerful vision that will direct and guide the change effort, and achieve the goals required. Following that they need to develop detailed strategies for achieving that vision. This might be done by each department or area of the organisation. The strategy needs to be:

- practical and workable on an operational level
- understandable and simple
- consistent across the organisation (one area's strategy should not undermine another elsewhere).

4. Communicating the change vision

A clear, powerful vision that is well communicated will:

- obtain people's understanding and hence their commitment
- initiate change throughout the organisation
- unlock people's energies and guide their actions, even in ways that the leader may not have anticipated.

To achieve this the leader needs to use every vehicle possible to communicate the new vision and strategies constantly. This will then start to build pressure, momentum and understanding, thereby sustaining a sense of urgency. In addition, the guiding coalition should lead by example and act as role models for the behaviour that is expected of employees.

5. Empowering broad-based action

The leader and the guiding coalition need to understand that they alone will not change their organisation: it needs to change from the grass-roots up and this can be best accomplished by allowing people to act in a blame-free and supportive environment.

To empower people the leader needs to:

- remove obstacles in the organisation
- change systems or structures that undermine the change vision
- encourage risk-taking and non-traditional ideas.

6. Generating short-term wins

Short-term wins are valuable in managing change because they:

- Highlight what is required and what the process means.
- Generate momentum for change.
- Provide an opportunity to build on success.

The leader should therefore:

- Plan for visible improvements in performance, or 'wins'.
- Create those wins.
- Visibly recognise and reward people who make the wins possible.

7. Consolidating gains and producing more change

In my experience this part of the process is the hardest: the excitement of the start-up phase has passed, the successes have been built and people know what is needed, but now they are tired and problems and difficulties continue to arise. The key is to move steadily: maintain momentum without moving too fast and destabilising the process. Inevitably it will take time. The leader needs to continue by:

- Using increased credibility and understanding of what is needed to change all systems, structures and policies that don't fit the vision.
- Hiring, promoting and developing people who can implement the change vision.
- Reinvigorating the process with new projects, themes and change agents.

8. Anchoring new approaches in the organisation's culture

One of the key dangers in managing change is to finish too soon. In fact, the best situation is often one where change, development and continuous improvements become the norm. What matters is ensuring that the changes are firmly grounded in the organisation. This requires the leader to explain the links between new behaviours and organisational success. It also requires that the leader prepares their successor to understand what has been gained, and where the process might go in the future.

Techniques for leading change

The following principles and techniques are useful when leading change:

1. *Empower people to effect change* – real change is achieved by everyone in the organisation acting together; empowerment is therefore an essential part of mobilising people to change.
2. *Communicate a sensible vision to employees* – if employees have a shared sense of purpose it will be easier to initiate actions to achieve that purpose.
3. *Ensure that the system does not hamper the vision for change* – the leader needs to remove any constraints (i.e. bureaucracy or procedures) that are incompatible with the vision and block needed action.

4. *Understand the need for training and development* – an inevitable result of the change process will be a need for training and development. The truth is that people will not be doing what they were before – or if they are, they will be doing it better. But to achieve this will probably require some action to increase their skills and ensure their personal development. The alternative is not to train, leaving people frustrated, without the right skills and attitudes, and disempowered.
5. *Ensure that all of the organisation's systems are in line with the new vision* – systems, such as personnel, finance, IT all need to be co-ordinated, providing the support that the new situation requires. If systems are out of step they will block action and cause frustration.
6. *Confront problems* – frustration is infectious, particularly when people are working hard or facing the unknown. It is vital therefore that the leader tackles any difficulties as soon as possible (ideally pre-empting them). This will show commitment and determination, as well as inspiring respect and confidence.

Summary: *Implementing and managing change*

Leading change is a vital aspect of leadership in general, because it requires dynamic, focused action. Without this proactive leadership, change will fail – or fail even to get started. Some of the key reasons why leadership is essential to delivering effective change are:

1. To provide vision – a clear idea of purpose and direction.
2. To communicate, facilitate, guide and focus activity.
3. To solve problems.
4. To co-ordinate and make decisions.
5. To motivate, encourage and support.

In general, to provide a framework that ensures success, including factors such as a sense of urgency, a need for quality, and a need for financial awareness.

Further information

Leading Change
John Kotter, Harvard Business School Press, 1996

Creating Culture Change
P. Atkinson, IFS Publications, 1990

Communication skills

Introduction

The ability to communicate clearly is an essential aspect of successful leadership, forming a vital element of almost every task. Leadership and management are about working productively through others, and of course this cannot be achieved without the ability to communicate. Consider for a moment the range of management activities where success or failure are often decided by the ability to communicate. These include delegation, negotiating, building high-performance teams, interviewing, conducting appraisals, setting objectives and deciding priorities, handling conflict, mentoring, motivating and empowering, leading change, decision-making, training and developing staff, global management, selling, meeting customer needs, building customer loyalty, unlocking creativity and innovation, managing and allocating resources, and so on.

Unfortunately communication skills are often overlooked: so important, so frequently used and so fundamental that they are taken for granted and often warrant little attention. Leaders frequently ignore the fact that communication skills can always be *improved*, with important benefits for the leader, the team and the success of the organisation as a whole.

Increasingly, the ability to communicate is linked to the ability to *influence* people. Indeed, they are often synonymous, and this blending of two concepts in 'management-speak' is (for once!) a good thing. It is good because *communicating* implies action and being directive, whereas *influencing* implies listening, understanding and channelling. In truth, both are vital components for successful communication.

The skills required for communicating to individuals differ in certain respects from those needed when communicating to groups. Clearly, many of the same skills are needed in both situations, such as an ability to understand the reaction that you are receiving, but there are also important differences. Just because you can rouse a crowd of 500 does not necessarily mean that you can make an impact on an individual! Similarly, many people are accomplished at leading individuals, but when it comes to instilling vision or directing action in a group – or just making a simple presentation – they are much less effective.

(For further information on this topic see *One Stop Communication* by David Martin.)

Checklist – understanding and influencing individuals

When communicating and influencing people there are a number of key skills that can be applied, and it is important not only to know *what* they are, but *when to use them* and *how to use them to best effect*. Communicating successfully therefore requires mastery of a range of skills and techniques; when communicating you should:

1. *Stop talking* – it is difficult to listen properly while you talk! Listening is the secret to communicating well as it enables you to:

    - understand the other person, empathise with them and ensure that you can address their concerns (for example, when handling conflict you need to listen and understand people's reactions, views and fears);
    - 'speak their language' and get your message across in terms they will understand and respond to;
    - build trust and respect. People are more likely to do what is asked of them if they can at least feel that they have had an opportunity to contribute and voice their own views;
    - focus on what people are *really* saying, not what you think they are saying.

2. *Empathise* – try to put yourself in the other person's position. This will help in understanding and overcoming their concerns, and keeping their commitment and motivation to you and the task.

3. *Remember to look out for body language* – both yours and theirs. Maintaining eye contact shows trust and interest, and observing their posture will give some idea of how they feel. Mirroring someone's body language sensitively is one way of helping to show that you are listening. Similarly, taking an aggressive posture (i.e. folding your arms or sitting side on to the other person) can show that your patience is wearing thin!

4. *Question* – asking questions not only improves your understanding but it can also test assumptions and show that you are listening. When asking questions you should also signal for attention: this will let the other person know that you want to comment and respond to their point, and allow them to pause and switch their attention to you before you speak.

5. *Summarise* – give an overview at the start of what you want to say, and finish by summarising what has been agreed. Summarising at key intervals also helps to prevent misunderstandings and move the conversation on to the next point.

6. *Maintain professionalism and control emotions* – professionalism can, of course, mean all things to all people! What is important is that you

should treat others as you would wish to be treated, for example don't interrupt, embarrass or be rude when communicating. Even if you feel it is the only way to make your point you should consider carefully whether it would ultimately undermine your position, and perhaps even your own self-esteem – it probably will. Controlling your emotions is also vitally important: you should avoid getting angry and instead stay in control.
7. *Ensure privacy and confidentiality, and remove distractions* – in order to maintain trust and to avoid rumours, misunderstandings and other unnecessary complications you should maintain confidentiality, especially with sensitive personnel issues. Removing distractions and avoiding interruptions will also show that you are serious and committed when communicating, and will help both parties concentrate and focus on the issues.
8. *Be critically aware* – this requires a variety of skills, in particular it means:

    - reacting to ideas, not people;
    - focusing on the significance to the discussion of the facts and evidence;
    - avoiding jumping to conclusions;
    - listening for *how* things are said, and what is *not* said. When talking to someone you need to be aware of their concerns and reactions, and to achieve this you need to create an environment where they can be honest and open. Even then, some people will still not say how they feel or what they think – or they may simply lack the skills to express themselves adequately. In these circumstances the leader needs to ask open, probing questions that will provide an indication of what the person is thinking.

9. *Avoid taking quick decisions* – give yourself time to think and react.
10. *Understand yourself* – recognise your own views and prejudices and avoid letting them influence your behaviour.
11. *Be sensitive and tactful, and in difficult situations choose your words carefully* – remember, if you disagree with what is being said don't start by saying that you disagree: this can often prompt a defensive or negative response. Instead, outline your views first and then explain why you disagree.

Communicating to groups

People tend to dislike giving presentations as they give rise to a number of concerns. Some of the difficulties include the feeling that it is hard to measure people's reactions; presenters worry about how they will be perceived, and feel that to speak at length to a group is somehow boastful or superior. Of course, all of these are arguments against leadership itself, not just presentations! Whilst group presentations can be tricky, even stressful, virtually all of the problems arise *before* the event. Successful leaders will prepare carefully and then deliver a confident – either informal or formal – presentation, the key being to take it in your stride and view it as you would any other aspect of leadership. Before you start preparing it is worth remembering that no two presenters are the same, and the best advice is generally to be yourself: comfortable, confident and relaxed.

When communicating to a group you should:

1. *Confirm the details.* With presentations the little things can be important; so, for example, make sure that you are the best person to deliver the presentation and you understand the content. You also need to ensure that you have enough time to prepare; you know what sort of presentation is expected (e.g. formal or informal); exactly what the topic and purpose of your presentation is; how long it is expected to last; whether there will be other speakers, and where and when you will be expected to give the presentation.
2. *Understand your audience.* You need to know what your audience is expecting – do they want to be informed, directed or given an opportunity to voice their own issues? How large will the audience be, and what is their level and background?

Case study: *The power of communication*

In the early 1980s British Airways was privatised at a time when the company was seen by many as a lame duck facing a range of difficult industrial and commercial problems, and without the safety net of government aid. In this situation the Chief Executive, Colin Marshall, undertook a bold and dynamic communications strategy that had the effect of reinvigorating the airline and its fortunes.

At the end of 1983 the staff awareness programme entitled *Putting People First* was launched, targeted at those 15,000 employees who had direct contact with customers. The programme communicated the vision and values of the business and its simple message inspired BA employees. The programme lasted two days and involved groups of up to 180: it was eventually extended to all of the airline's employees and ran for two and a half years. Colin Marshall personally gave the closing address at 40 per cent of

COMMUNICATION SKILLS

> the seminars, and where he was unable to another senior BA executive would take his place.
>
> This programme was followed by several other total employee programmes, such as *Managing People First*, a one-week programme that concentrated on leadership; *A Day in the Life, which* outlined the quality and scope of the company's operations; *To be the Best*, which focused on competition in world markets, and *Winners*, which emphasised quality and customer service. Other programmes are currently ongoing.
>
> The effects of this group communication strategy have been significant. Against expectations and in a highly competitive market BA became established as one of the world's leading airline companies. Much of this success can be attributed to the effectiveness of the company's communication and development programmes, which have had the following effects:
>
> - Empowering and motivating staff.
> - Fostering initiative and innovation, and unlocking employees' potential.
> - Helping to change the culture of the organisation into a dynamic and customer-oriented business.
> - Reinforcing the company's sales message that it is a market leader.
> - Gaining the support and respect of key stakeholders, such as suppliers, government and financial institutions.

3. *Prepare and rehearse.* When preparing your presentation you should tailor it to meet the needs of your audience. You will therefore need to:

- *Define the purpose* – is it to persuade, instruct, inspire and motivate, challenge or entertain? What is your message going to be?
- *Assemble, organise and structure your material* – make sure that you have a beginning, middle and an end, and see whether there are themes or analogies that appear regularly. You may wish to write your speech out on cue cards, or possibly use an autocue for major, formal presentations.
- *Prepare and refine your draft* – review the draft speech, and refine it by running through it, preferably in front of someone. Feedback on content, style and delivery are all important.

- *Decide on visual aids (and any prompts that you may need)* – aids need to be appropriate, simple and clear to understand, and flow from your natural style. You also need to make sure that you have mastered them!
- *Rehearse* – this can include everything from running through the presentation in your head, to delivering it in front of your partner! Watch out for any distracting mannerisms, or points to remember such as 'smile', and where to pause for emphasis. Also, it may be worth trying to anticipate likely questions.
- *Check the venue* – make sure that you feel comfortable and relaxed in advance of the event.

4. *Choose the right words.* A number of techniques can be used to deliver a powerful, successful presentation. All of them fulfil the aims of the talk: to interest, inform and persuade.

    - *Choose words that your audience will understand* – clarity is fundamental to keeping the audience interested. Choose your vocabulary to ensure the audience understands your points but is not patronised. Explain any unavoidable technical terms or jargon if you think the audience will not understand them.
    - *Choose words that emphasise your points and impact on the audience* – repetition can add emphasis to a point; alliteration and onomatopoeia add impact. Also, where appropriate, don't be afraid to use emotive words or phrases to appeal to the audience – this forces them to react and think about what you are saying. Also, rhetorical questions make your audience think about the point.
    - *Remember the 'rule of three'* – give three examples of your point in the same sentence. For example: *journalists have to be hardworking, tenacious and trustworthy!*
    - *Use a variety of interesting words and good descriptions* – avoid using the same expressions over and over – use a thesaurus.
    - *Choose words for structure and clarity.* Use connective words that help your talk flow and allow the audience to follow your argument easily e.g.: *therefore, for example, on the other hand, consequently, in addition, furthermore, finally, in conclusion.*

5. *Start and finish.* The way that you open and close your talk is vitally important to success. It is worth spending time on this to get it right.

    - *The opening* sets the tone and capture the audience's attention. The opening should make it clear what the talk is about and what you hope to achieve.

COMMUNICATION SKILLS

- *The closing* leaves the audience with a final impression. The closing should draw the main points together and impact on the audience.

6. *Final review.* Before delivering the presentation it is wise to check that you are prepared:

    - Have you researched the topic thoroughly?
    - Is the talk interesting, informative and persuasive?
    - Is your talk well structured, clear and understandable?
    - Are you appealing directly to the audience, both in content and style of delivery?
    - Do you have a good opening and strong closing?

7. *Delivering the presentation.* The way that you speak is called the register. The register you choose will depend on the audience, the aim of your talk and the topic in question. Use a tone and style appropriate to the audience and topic. Silence can also be a powerful weapon. Speakers can get extremely anxious over the slightest of pauses, and talk rapidly and incoherently to avoid the silence. Only practice and confidence can overcome this obstacle. The most adept speakers use silence to hold the audience's attention: it forces them to focus on the speaker, and makes them keen to hear the next point. Other points to remember include:

    - *Slow down.* You know the topic: the audience needs time to absorb the points.
    - *Speak clearly and distinctly*; speak to the back of the audience.
    - *Look at the audience.* Be confident: they want to listen to you.
    - *Speak with expression.* Stress points that are important and keep the tone of your voice appropriate to the subject matter.
    - *Use moderate repetition* to emphasise your point.
    - *Pause for effect.*
    - *Don't rush* – you'll lose the audience.
    - *Don't hesitate or mumble*, and avoid using 'em' or 'er'.
    - *Don't use slang* or colloquialisms – a speech is a formal occasion.
    - *Don't use too many gestures.*
    - *Relax.* Breathe steadily, and enjoy yourself.

Summary: *Effective communication*

Being able to speak well in different situations is central to the successful promotion of your ideas. Many leaders find public speaking a daunting and nerve-wracking experience. Preparation, understanding the key features of effective speaking and using a variety of techniques will result in a well-presented and well-received talk. These skills can also be used for other types of situation such as interviews, negotiations or selling.

In addition, throughout the preparation, writing and delivery of presentations it is important to understand what makes for success. A good speech must:

- Introduce the audience to the topic using interesting arguments and examples.
- Enlighten the audience with clear explanations.
- Hold the audience throughout by maintaining an interesting and appealing style.
- Influence the audience through persuasive techniques.

Further information

Tough Talking – How to handle awkward situations
D. Martin, FT/Pitman, 1996

One Stop Communication
D. Martin, ICSA Publishing, 1999

The Handbook of Presentation Skills
B. Hurst, Kogan Page, 1996

Successful Presentations in a Week
M. Peel, Hodder Headline, 1998

Creativity and innovation

Introduction

Leadership is about getting the best from people, yet it is only recently that the creative talent of people at work has been seen as a major asset that needs to be unlocked. There are two key dimensions to creativity and innovation:

1. *The fact that everyone has the capacity for creativity.* This has been highlighted by research as well as being demonstrated in practice, and it is worth remembering that outside work individuals can be hugely creative – why not harness those skills at work? Indeed, to be fully motivated and achieve success people often need to realise their creative potential.
2. *Organisations increasingly require creativity and innovation for success* – not simply to keep up with the rapid pace of change, competition and new opportunities, but also to solve problems and to make the best decisions.

This section provides an understanding of the importance of creativity and innovation, and outlines techniques for leaders to use to unlock their team's creative potential.

Techniques for encouraging creativity

Understanding creativity

To develop creative skills and foster innovation, leaders need to build the right environment and help team members to practise being creative. Creativity can be displayed in a variety of ways:

1. *Practical and motor skills* – these are the skills of the craftworker or athlete.
2. *Visual skills* – these are skills used in art and design.
3. *Intellectual skills* – these are the cognitive skills which are usually of greatest relevance at work, as they are the skills that help people to manipulate concepts and ideas, solve problems, create opportunities and add value.

Neuroscience divides creativity into *left brain activities*, which are logical and analytical, and *right brain activities*, which are creative and integrative. A systematic approach to creativity is provided by Edward de Bono who has distinguished between *vertical thinking*, which is bounded by logic and linear thinking, and *lateral thinking*, which cuts across normal boundaries and processes. De Bono's theory, which is hugely popular and widely adopted, is that there are many problems that are not easily solved by traditional modes of thinking: in these situations lateral thinking is useful for generating new ideas and approaches.

- One of the essential features of lateral thinking is combining ideas and concepts that have not previously been combined.
- Another aspect is removing binding assumptions by asking *what if?* questions.

An illustration of this approach is Einstein's theory of relativity, which resulted from him cycling around northern Italy in his twenties and asking the question: 'What would happen if I could travel on a beam of light?'

Factors preventing creativity

Understanding the factors preventing creativity is vital in eliminating them. They include:

- lack of confidence
- fear of failure
- perfectionism and self-criticism
- fear of how being creative will appear to others
- resistance to change
- fear of uncertainty and ambiguity
- organisational cultures that include negativity or blame
- rigid organisational structures.

In addition there may be many other specific factors relevant to each organisation and individual.

Mind mapping

This is a technique for organising thoughts and ideas into a clear form, from which patterns, ideas and new approaches will emerge or crystallise. Mind maps also help to clarify issues and share and communicate ideas in a powerful way. They can include:

- Listing thoughts into pros and cons.

CREATIVITY AND INNOVATION

- *Grouping issues into specific categories* – the most popular example being SWOT analysis (identifying internal Strengths and Weaknesses and external Opportunities and Threats).
- *Displaying ideas in diagrammatic form*, such as spider diagrams, flowcharts, fishbone diagrams, matrix boxes, graphs and cycles, which can help to highlight relationships between ideas.

Brainstorming

This is a technique, usually led by a facilitator, in which a group of people are encouraged to give vent to all their ideas on a specific topic. The atmosphere is one of constructive suggestion rather than commentary or criticism. After ideas have been generated they are discussed, explored and prioritised – perhaps creating new solutions using elements from several suggestions.

Case study: *Brainstorming innovations*

A manager ran a brainstorming session and was looking for ideas for a new service that was being developed. The session was planned to cover the following issues: a title for the new service, marketing ideas and a pricing structure. The manager that was organising the session was the product champion and was closely involved in all aspects of the project; in fact, because of the manager's style – he preferred working on his own and providing written reports as appropriate – few people knew much about the service at all.

When the session started people were completely uninformed about the service and their role in the session. By the time this had been fully explained the views of the manager were clear, and when the time came to invite ideas people were, not surprisingly, quite quiet. A few brave souls suggested some ideas and were either patronised or rejected, and as this painful process continued the group gradually ganged up against the manager. The session achieved little except ill-will and frustration.

With this experience in mind, another manager organised a similar brainstorming event several weeks later, with much the same purpose, albeit for a

> different project. The preparation was good, the session went well and a steady flow of ideas was generated. Participants left feeling much better – however, the manager at the second session had failed to ask participants to prioritise or discard many of the ideas that had been generated. As a result, there was a wealth of ideas but little guidance on how they could be interrelated or combined into an effective whole. Indeed, some of the brightest ideas had been thought of already, and discarded because of cost or timing.
>
> Without proper preparation, organisation and follow-through during the brainstorming sessions neither one realised their full potential, and the sessions ultimately gave little more than legitimacy to decisions reached elsewhere.

Checklist – fostering innovation

Teams are often constrained by traditional boundaries, and this is further reinforced by individuals' own experiences which lead many people to think in terms of functional boxes. Innovation is about thinking *outside of these boxes*, forgetting the boundaries and achieving breakthrough solutions and ideas. To foster innovation leaders can undertake the following activities.

Encourage a questioning approach

The leader needs to establish a culture that is free of cynicism or blame and that encourages questioning. Team members should be permitted and encouraged to:

- Question perceived, established logic – and ask *why?*
- Question the limits of existing processes, systems or technology.
- Identify false assumptions.

Questioning may not by itself provide breakthrough thinking, but it is an essential first step in breaking traditional thinking.

Understand that good ideas may come from a range of sources

It is tempting for leaders to think that good ideas should reflect the hierarchy of the organisation, i.e. the more senior, experienced or well paid someone is, the more likely they are to come up with an innovation. Whilst this may be true of certain industries, it is probably only relevant in so far as seniority reflects *confidence*. In other words, there may be excellent ideas in unusual places – junior members of staff, competitors, other industries, historical legend – and the leader needs to be open to all approaches. For example, the British Post Office saved millions of pounds and helped their staff and customers enormously by printing 'first' and 'second' on their first-class and second-class stamps, instead of a postage price which was liable to change. This idea, so the story goes, was suggested by a junior post-room employee.

Focus on what is required

It often helps for the leader to focus the team on the needs of the organisation. These might include:

- The needs and preferences of customers (internal and external)
- The strategic aims of the organisation
- The team and individual objectives
- Guideline vision statements and goals
- Benchmarking information from competitors as well as other industries.

Continue removing constraints and driving innovation

The leader should exert some pressure and rigour on the process of innovation to avoid casual drift and the dissipation of ideas by:

- Setting tight deadlines.
- Not limiting thinking to feasible options – radical change and re-engineering may be necessary.
- Putting past experience in context: just because it has never happened before does not mean it can never succeed in the future.
- Using to the full the resources that are available – notably data, information technology and the views and experience of others.
- Giving praise and credit where and when they are due. This can help to ensure that the process continues successfully, that people remain motivated and that the successful idea gathers momentum.

Ensure that innovations are grounded in reality

Innovative ideas need to be tested, planned and related to the practical realties of a situation. It may well be that the people that generated the ideas are not necessarily the best ones to check the practical implications – or maybe they are the *only* ones to do this! It obviously depends on the people and the situations involved. It is worth the leader considering the various personality types within the team and deciding how best (and who) should develop the ideas. (See TEAM-BUILDING AND DEVELOPING HIGH-PER-FORMING TEAMS, for further information.)

> **Summary:** *The importance of decisive leadership*
>
> New ideas can often fail because of poor planning and execution. This may result from the fact that the skills needed to generate breakthrough thinking are vision and an overall view, whereas successful implementation can often require attention to detail and process skills. Even when ideas are successfully implemented and work, they can fall apart if they are not monitored, evaluated, refined and generally embedded in the organisation. Again, this can require patient, critical analysis.
>
> Finally, innovations and ideas can be lost due to a lack of courage, conviction or decisiveness, or by analysing the idea to death. The leader needs to act *decisively*, investigating it positively if it seems worthwhile, or else dismissing it on the basis of sound reasoning rather than prejudice or instinct.

Further information

Effective Innovation
J. Adair, Pan, 1996

Creativity at Work
T. Rickards, Gower, 1988

Successful Problem-Solving: the organised approach to creative solutions
D.F. Juniper, Foulsham, 1989

Decision-making

Introduction

Many people view decision-making as the essence of leadership, and certainly the ability to make the best decisions consistently remains one of the defining skills of a leader in any situation. Decision-making is deceptive: it can seem straightforward to understand the essentials of a problem or situation and then decide what to do next, however reality is seldom like that. Decision-making actually involves a range of skills linked into a clear, practical process, including:

- analysing and appraising competing options
- communicating and influencing
- fostering innovation and creativity
- exploiting synergies
- managing information and knowledge
- focusing on the customer and understanding market needs
- leading change
- resolving problems effectively.

This section outlines the basic skills needed for effective decision-making; the process in which they can be applied, and the hidden traps in decision-making.

The decision-making process

Getting the decision right has six key elements:

1. Clearly defining the objective
2. Collecting and analysing relevant information
3. Developing practical options
4. Evaluating the options and deciding what to do
5. Implementing the decision
6. Monitoring the effects and, if necessary, repeating the process.

Clearly defining the objective

It is often difficult to define a clear objective when there are a number of competing priorities, but there are several possible approaches:

- Decide which objective offers the greatest number of potential benefits or simply which is the most important. One technique is to ask *why* this is important, what benefits does it bring.
- Refer to existing policies or plans (e.g. a strategic business plan) to see what objective offers the greatest overall benefit.
- Seek the views of others and try to gain a consensus about what the objective should be.
- Test hypotheses and ideas, i.e. if this was the objective what would be the likely decision, and what would be the possible outcome.

Collecting and analysing relevant information

There are several questions to ask in order to ensure you have all of the necessary information:

- Do you know *what* information is required to reach a good decision?
- Do you have all the necessary information and expertise to make a quality decision?
- If not, do you know who does have the relevant information or where it can be found?
- Can you rely on others to help with this decision? Is it reasonable?
- Would experience be relevant in making this decision?

Analysing relevant information can be even harder. The following techniques are often relevant:

- Understand and organise the facts, separating them from assumptions or opinions.
- Understand the nature of the problem by asking: who, what, why, when, where and how?
- Breaking the whole into its component parts works for complex matters. This means finding the root cause of the problem, working from first principles and identifying the *either/or* on which many decisions rest.

Developing practical options

These can be achieved by:

- Analysing the information and reviewing the possible paths to the desired outcome.
- Seeking the views of others and brainstorming ideas.
- Using creativity and conceptual thinking to imagine possible scenarios and solutions.

Evaluating the options and deciding what to do

The leader needs to evaluate the available options by considering a number of key questions:

- What are the risks and potential barriers to success?
- How attractive are the options? (For a commercial organisation this might often be in the form: how *financially* attractive are the options?)
- Which decisions are possible, and of those, which are *feasible*?
- Do the feasible options need to be reduced to one decision, or could a combination of decisions be taken?
- When is action required? Now, later or not at all?
- What action might be needed to keep options open for the future.

The decision needs to be in line with the objective(s) and overall strategy, and should be consistent with other decisions and policies. In reaching a decision the leader should consider:

- Deciding what the desired outcome would be, and working backwards to find the decision most likely to bring it about.
- Asking whether the problem can really help to solve another problem or issue.
- Taking a view of the whole area, rather than just the narrow decision that needs to be made.

Case study: *Avoiding paralysis by analysis*

A business was on the verge of launching a major new product – a modern, stylish table lamp that was distinctive and used new technology that was inexpensive and simulated daylight. The product manager knew that it would appeal to a wide range of markets, including households, offices and businesses, and it could sell through a range of channels including retailers and wholesalers, as well as through direct response advertising. The difficulty faced by the marketing manager was that the company was short of money to spend on marketing and the new product was seen as the company's great hope and salvation.

Anxious not to get the launch wrong, the company researched, discussed and refined its plans many times. But as the launch date drew nearer the key decisions about pricing and marketing spend were still

> not being resolved. People were too afraid of getting the key decisions wrong, and for every possible alternative there were risks, costs and adverse consequences.
>
> The deadlock was broken by a young manager – not the most senior person involved at all, but someone who had a clear vision of how the product could succeed. He developed a marketing plan and passionately sold their ideas to each person involved, one by one. The plan was clear – it segmented the markets, reduced the risk by spreading it across several markets, and included fall-back positions should sales not go as expected. But most of all the plan was owned, and the views held were, with only minor modifications, clearly held. Senior managers were relieved that the initiative had been seized and supported the plan completely. When it was implemented it met with reasonable success: strong in certain markets, weak in others. Changes were made and the business evolved so that from a modest start the product became market leader within twelve months.
>
> The need for a determined, decisive start is paramount: almost inevitably there will be problems, but it became apparent to the manager taking the initiative that what was needed was action and as much support as possible. Then when changes are needed, as they inevitably are, there is the support to carry them through and build on what has gone before – whether success or failure.

Implementing the decision

There is a danger that many leaders see decision-making as an end in itself, rather than a means to an end (the objective). It is vital that the practical implementation of the decision is fully considered – the who, where, how and when – and that this is understood and acted on by the leader. Also, there is little point in reaching decisions if others misunderstand them, as this can lead to decisions being poorly implemented and failing. Communicating and implementing decisions so that they achieve what is intended often implies influencing people and gaining support.

Monitoring the effects and, if necessary, repeating the process

Making a decision and then sticking with it is often important, but needs to be tempered with an ability to recognise when the situation has moved on and a new decision is required. Monitoring the effects of the decision will also provide useful information for its continued implementation and success, as well as for future decisions.

Checklist – essential techniques for effective decision-making

1. *Trust your judgement and accept responsibility.*
2. *Avoid paralysis by analysis* – analysis is vital, but so is reaching and implementing the decision. Leaders need to have an awareness of any time constraints and the consequences of delay, and they also need to possess the courage to decide.
3. *Avoid hasty or quick decisions* – there can be a tendency for some people to work from intuition or experience, and quickly decide the best course of action. Clearly this may work in instances where, for example, experience is paramount, but careful analysis and thought may provide an even better decision – as well as potentially avoiding a disaster!
4. *Manage the risk in decision-making* – when it is time to make the decision it may be worth considering whether the situation is low-risk or high-risk; whether failure will be costly if it is high-risk, and if other people need to be involved in making – or approving – the decision. There may be reasons to be risk-averse, but fear of failure should not be one of them.
5. *Consider the wider impact of decisions, particularly on corporate culture.* Nurturing and influencing the right organisational culture is important for many leaders in achieving success, yet many of the key decisions affecting corporate culture are trivialised, rushed or taken in isolation. The effects of business culture permeate the organisation: they impact on issues as diverse as recruitment and retention of staff; personnel and office costs; suppliers' attitudes and performance, and even how the business brand is perceived by customers. The leader therefore needs to:

    - Be aware of the effect on corporate culture of their strategic decisions.
    - Build an environment that routinely takes the best decisions, using a clearly defined process but where possible allowing for innovation and initiative.

6. *Ensure thorough analysis and entrepreneurial decisions* – common denominators of a successful business are its people, products, markets, profit and cash flow. Whilst there is a tendency to focus on decisions affecting the first three, there is often fear and neglect surrounding financial skills and decisions. It is important to complete each stage of the decision-making process thoroughly, and for major commercial decisions this may well involve using financial techniques such as forecasting or ratio analysis.

> **Summary:** *Avoiding the hidden traps in decision-making*
>
> Bad decisions can often be traced to the way the decisions were made: the alternatives were not clearly defined; the right information was not collected; the costs and benefits were not accurately weighed. But sometimes the fault lies not in the decision-making process, *but in the mind of the decision-maker*: The way that the human brain works can sabotage the choices we make. Research in the United States has identified traps that are particularly likely to affect the way that strategic business decisions are made:
>
> 1. *The anchoring trap* leads us to give disproportionate weight to the first information that we receive. This often happens because of the initial impact of the first information and our immediate reaction to it. The antidote is to be sure about what is happening and waiting as long as possible to ensure that you have all the information – and possibly some different options too.
> 2. *The status quo trap* biases us towards maintaining the current situation – even when better alternatives exist. This might be caused by inertia, or the potential loss of face if the current position was to change. The only solutions are openness, honesty and courage.
> 3. *The sunk-cost trap* inclines us to perpetuate the mistakes of the past on the grounds that 'we have invested so much in this approach/decision that we cannot abandon it or alter course now'. The

management accountant's view of this is refreshingly sanguine: if it's spent it's spent – worry about the present and future, not the past.

Avoiding the following traps requires recognising that they exist and understanding which traps are most likely to cause you problems, as well as adhering to each of the stages in the decision-making process.

4. *The confirming-evidence trap* results in our seeking out information to support an existing predilection and to discount opposing information.
5. *The framing trap* is when we incorrectly state a problem, totally undermining the decision making process. This is often unintentional, but not always ...
6. *The over-confidence trap* makes us overestimate the accuracy of our forecasts.
7. *The prudence trap* leads us to be over-cautious when we make estimates about uncertain factors.

Realism, perhaps erring on the side of caution (depending on the nature of the decision), is the antidote to 6 and 7.

8. *The recent event trap* leads us to give undue weight to a recent, and quite probably dramatic event (or sequence of events). This is very similar to the anchoring trap, except that it can arise at any time, not just at the start, and cause a misjudgement. Awareness of the trap and the danger that it might pose for you in the way you think is vital for avoiding it.

Further information

The New Rational Manager
C.H. Kepner and B.B. Tregoe, John Martin, 1981

Decision-Making: An integrated approach
D. Jennings and S. Wattam, FT/Pitman, 1994

Problem-Solving and Decision-Making
G. Wilson, Kogan Page, 1993

Effective Decision-Making: A practical guide for management
H. Drummond, Kogan Page, 1993

Delegating effectively

Introduction

Delegation is the act of giving someone the authority to make decisions and act in a specified area of work. In giving someone else the authority to act on your behalf you must accept that you are at the same time giving them the 'right' to be wrong. Given the excessive workloads of many managers, learning to delegate is a vital skill to master. Delegation is best seen as a personal skill rather than a job task. It is one of the keys to personal effectiveness, making you and your team more productive and successful.

To delegate effectively the leader must recognise that certain activities must belong to them; others can be shared and some even relinquished. The activities which the leader undertakes must be those which only they can do, and usually include policy-making and planning, people management, evaluation and conflict resolution. Learning to delegate requires the leader to think about the team, where previously they may have only considered their own work and tasks.

The *direct* advantages of successful delegation are greater productivity and better use of resources. However, the *indirect* benefits are no less significant for the individual, the organisation and the team members. These might include better time management and reduced stress; greater understanding leading to process improvements and innovation; improved decision-making; greater motivation, and reduced staff turnover.

Respect and clarity underpin effective delegation. Leaders should treat others as they would wish to be treated themselves, and this is particularly true when delegating.

The benefits of delegation

Delegation allows decisions to be taken at the level where the details are known, and it reduces delays in decision-making – as long as authority is delegated close to the point of action. There are a number of other key benefits:

For the organisation there is:

- better use of the leader's time, which is expensive;
- an opportunity to develop skills and experience in subordinates. This in turn provides motivation in individuals through achievement;
- full use of the team's skills by fully analysing what they can do;
- the development of trained, competent understudies who are ready to step in and provide support when required.

For the leader there is:

- relief from routine and less critical tasks, extending the capacity to manage;
- more time to stand back from the 'hurly burly' of the present and to think and plan for the future. This includes time to plan to avoid problems – and time to deal with them if they occur!
- better time and stress management as a result.

For the team there is:

- increasing confidence that comes from greater competence;
- more scope to use different skills, and many more development opportunities;
- greater interest, involvement and job satisfaction throughout the team.

What to delegate

Leaders delegate tasks that they don't need to do themselves. Delegation is not about getting rid of the difficult, tedious or unrewarding tasks. Delegation may, in fact, make the leader's life *more* complicated, but also more rewarding and successful. As a leader you should certainly delegate routine and repetitive tasks which you cannot reasonably be expected to do yourself; and you must then use the time you have gained productively.

You should also delegate specialist tasks to those who have the skills and know-how to do them. You have to know how to select and use expertise: make it clear what you want from the experts, and ask them to present it to you in a usable way.

Think about your job, listing all of the things you do and decide:

- What must you do yourself?
- What could others do with my help?
- What could others do better than me?
- What must others do?
- To whom would you delegate? And what tasks would you give each person?
- What would you do with the extra time?

What to avoid delegating

There are some tasks that cannot be delegated. Each individual needs to consider their own job and decide which tasks they must do themselves. In choosing areas of work to delegate you must act with discretion. A good rule of thumb is to avoid the following general areas:

1. *Policy-making and goal-setting* – these are key areas for managers to focus on and not usually delegated.
2. *Specific people management issues,* such as discipline, appraisal, dispute resolution are also best dealt with by managers.
3. *Major external issues,* such as crisis management or legal action.

There are certain activities that normally only someone with the status of a manager can undertake. Leaders should always avoid delegating the following tasks:

- delegation
- coaching, counselling and morale issues
- appraisals, performance evaluations and feedback
- disciplinary proceedings
- confidential tasks and sensitive situations
- planning and management
- complex situations
- tasks which have been specifically assigned.

Key steps in successful delegation

There are a number of key stages in successful delegation:

1. *Preparing to delegate.* Focus on the results that you want to achieve and have clear, precise objectives. This may require careful consideration and planning, and possibly discussion with other colleagues. You may also need to give some thought to priorities: What should come first? Is the work piling up on *everyone*? If this is the case, then delegation may not be the solution. Always consider the *importance* and *urgency* of the task that you are delegating.
2. *Matching person and task.* To delegate effectively we need to be able to identify which of our daily tasks could be tackled by other people. The person who is being required to do the job must understand it and have the personal skills and competence to tackle it, even if it is different, important and challenging.
3. *Discuss and agree objectives.* The task, from the purpose through to the fulfilment, should be talked through. Having allocated tasks you need to agree targets, objectives, resources, review times and deadlines. (It is worth remembering that when setting objectives they should always be

SMART: Specific, Measurable, Achievable, Results-related/Realistic and Time-constrained.) Be sure to check understanding and gain explicit agreement to your plan.
4. *Provide resources and the appropriate level of authority.* Make sure that you provide all the necessary resources, the authority to complete the task and give all the necessary back-up. Define responsibilities clearly and be there to advise when appropriate. Always follow up your actions and plan how you will monitor and control events.
5. *Monitor progress.* Delegation without control is abdication. This does not mean interfering when there is no need, but control does mean checking progress at pre-planned and specified times. Control also involves verifying that things are on track. Monitoring and control ensure that the delegated task is completed successfully and that the desired results are achieved. The key to monitoring is to ensure that the person completing the task remains accountable.
6. *Review and assess overall performance.* This is best done by checking achievements against the original objectives.

Developing the right attitudes for successful delegation

Delegating successfully depends on many different factors: the type of job, the work environment, the experience of the employee, the timing of the situation and the degree of understanding between the manager and team member. A key element in delegating successfully, and finding a way through all these different factors, is to *develop the right attitude*: it is only then that you are likely to generate the right attitude in others.

The right attitudes when delegating are *positive* ones. They include:

- showing confidence and personal security by letting go;
- showing trust;
- being prepared to take risks and support mistakes;
- being patient;
- obtaining commitment;
- being task-oriented.

Letting go

Good delegators feel confident in their abilities and position in the organisation and have a positive attitude to delegating. Delegating is viewed as a way of preparing team members to be future managers. Above all, good, confident delegators view it as a means of achieving their own, and the company's, goals. This confidence is necessary because it will help you to have the courage to let someone else perform a task that you would normally do, while still accepting full responsibility for the outcome.

Many managers have difficulty letting go because they are afraid that others will do something dreadful that they would never have done themselves. If this is you, then you need to remind yourself that:

- You are not the only person capable of doing what you do.
- It does not matter if the job is done differently from the way that you would do it, as long as it is done to the required standard.
- You will not lose control of your work if you let go of a part of it.

Showing trust

When delegating, a good manager needs to trust another person to perform a task for which the manager alone will be held responsible. This requires deep and resilient reserves of trust on both sides, and a positive attitude from the start. To develop trust during delegation remember the following do's and don'ts:

1. *Do back up team members' decisions* – even if you don't agree with them back them up when they need support, and always in front of others. Guiding, coaching and counselling are far more effective when delegating than criticism, negativity and disagreement.
2. *Don't dwell on mistakes* – people usually know when they have made a mistake and you should always try to give the person the opportunity to correct it.
3. *Do be clear about your expectations* – share your expectations with team members in advance.
4. *Don't undermine people* – an important rule at any time and never more so than when delegating. This includes avoiding withholding information or spying on your team. Instead of spying, agree clear guidelines for monitoring progress and then stick to them.
5. *Do be honest and open* – hiding information or your own mistakes, even inadvertently, can cause mistrust or resentment. Share information with team members so that they can perform their job, and be straightforward with them. Don't, for instance, manipulate people with implied rewards or pressure them with guilt. In short, show them respect and courtesy.
6. *Do examine assumptions* – make sure that you are making the right assumptions. If someone succeeds or fails, was it the result of what they did? If they are reluctant to undertake the task is it for a reason you understand, or could it be because of something else?

Taking risks and supporting mistakes

The best leaders are those that are willing to take risks in order to get things done: they are prepared to stretc.h resources and make mistakes, and are

> **Case study:** *The power of trust*
>
> A manager was appointed to a head a major business centre for a large, reputable academic organisation. Although the manager was experienced in many areas it was her first experience of profit-centre management. In her first year she had a number of notable successes: the profile and reputation of the organisation was enhanced, innovative products and services were developed, and standards in areas such as customer service were raised as a direct result of her actions. However, this was achieved at a cost: in the first year the 'profit-centre' made a loss of £50,000 (a sum that was significant relative to other parts of the organisation).
>
> The manager was extremely disappointed, although she was hardly surprised as the monthly management accounts had made the impending loss evident for nearly six months. The reaction of her director, however, was surprising: rather than reduce her responsibilities or take other drastic action (which she expected), his response was simply to make it clear that such a situation was unacceptable and should not occur again. He told her to discuss the monthly management accounts with him for the next few months and to raise any significant financial decisions either with him or the management accountant. Several weeks later it formed only a small part of her annual appraisal as it had already been discussed, one outcome being the need for financial training. The manager was relieved and determined to improve on this weakness, and keen to demonstrate that her director's trust was not misplaced. The business improved its financial position the following year and the manager was a better, more careful, experienced and successful individual as a result.

always willing to accept and learn from failure. You do not want people to make mistakes if they can help it, but inevitably they will happen. It is important that people know that if something goes wrong they can admit it: this establishes a positive attitude and encourages team members not to let you down. If support and a 'no blame' atmosphere is not present then the person doing the work will be cautious, distracted, and may ultimately turn a mistake into a crisis by hiding it from you.

Being patient

When you delegate you should be aware that results take time. Remember:

- Allow team members the chance to develop their own judgement by using their own methods.
- If a project falls behind schedule, make sure that the team member has a plan for getting it back on track. Don't panic and take over the project.
- Allow time to *explain* what is required and *agree* what needs to happen (i.e. when you will monitor progress).

Obtaining commitment

You need to be certain that when you delegate a task it is being received with commitment; the people completing it need to be interested, willing and able. Ability without willingness and commitment is nothing: one volunteer is worth a hundred coerced employees. Gaining commitment can take time, but it is absolutely essential. To obtain commitment you need to persuade people that:

- The task they are completing is necessary and worthwhile, however small.
- They have the freedom to decide how to work, as long as the objectives are met.
- They have been given the task because they are considered capable of completing it, stretching their abilities and increasing their self-esteem and self-confidence.

Being task-oriented and keeping control

When delegating, remember to focus on the tasks that are being completed. Effective delegation means that you need to establish a means of control including *channels* for reporting progress and problems (consider using review meetings, progress reports), and a *schedule* for when reporting should take place.

If you are unhappy with the amount of feedback and control, you should do two things: establish additional means for monitoring progress, and tell the team member that you are going to follow up frequently on the project's progress. You don't need to make a big issue out of this, nor should it stop you appearing confident and positive about the final outcome: you're just concerned to make sure it stays on track and you can provide support when needed. This warning and dialogue will help to remove any feelings of interference or meddling.

Matching people to tasks

Getting the best match between person and task is vitally important. When you delegate it is worth remembering:

- to assess the capabilities of each person individually;
- what motivates people, what they like and each person's workload;
- to be clear about the level of authority you are giving the person;
- to be clear about what you expect the person to do and, if relevant, how you expect the task to be completed. Are there key points or milestones? Do you expect the person to update you regularly? Who deals with problems? When must it be completed?

There are a number of ways of matching tasks to people, and to a large extent the right technique depends on the scale and complexity of the task as much as the attitude of the manager. Some people will always delegate and assign work on the basis of intuition, or possibly just reflex. Others always take a scientific view, listing criteria and scoring people against particular qualities and requirements. Both approaches are right and the effective leader is the one that develops their own style of delegating which is routine, appropriate, comfortable and effective for all involved.

Checklist – delegating to the best person

Key questions to consider when deciding who to delegate to are:

1. What exactly does the job involve – and are there any specific problem areas?
2. Who would expect to do the job – does it 'belong' to a person or position?
3. Who is trained to do the job?
4. Who has the interest and ability to complete the task?
5. Who would benefit from the experience of completing the task?
6. Who is available?
7. Who has been neglected in the past? (And who is least busy?)
8. Would the task help anyone to improve their ability for a new position or promotion?

Overcoming problems when delegating

Adequate preparation is vital for successful delegation. Many difficulties arise because managers take a simplistic view of delegation, seeing it as no more than asking 'Will you do this job for me?'

Common problems when preparing to delegate include:

Delegating the wrong type of task

If you don't consider carefully what it is that you are asking your colleagues to do, how and when they will do it and how successful they are likely to be, then you are taking a huge risk. Think clearly about the task first, make sure it can be delegated and consider any other implications – for example, how will other colleagues view it, both inside and outside your team?

Delegating without planning, preparation or sufficient time

Tasks may be delegated incorrectly, to the wrong person and often come back to the manager anyway, unfinished and in a worse state than at the start. Time and stress pressures may build up, trust may be reduced and the manager may not be able to find someone to do the job. Think carefully about delegating tasks and set time aside to delegate properly. It may take time but it saves more.

Only delegating unpleasant tasks

The quickest way to lose respect and authority as a manager is to only delegate boring, trivial or unpleasant tasks, whilst at the same time keeping the enjoyable or visible tasks. Assignments should include both enjoyable and unpleasant tasks, equally divided among team members according to skills, abilities and fairness.

Overlapping tasks and responsibilities

Problems can arise when two or more individuals are responsible for doing the same task. This often means that work assignments are too general or that different jobs have overlapping responsibilities. Quite apart from being inefficient it is usually very annoying and frustrating to the people involved. The solution is to define clearly who does what, specifically outlining responsibilities; if necessary, it may also help to get those involved together to agree who will do what.

Checklist – signs that delegation may not be working

- team members are always too busy
- low morale
- excessive arguments and 'political' difficulties, either within your team or between teams
- productivity declines
- mistakes increase
- deadlines are not being met
- team members are frequently surprised by your actions: what you are doing and what you expect of them..
- team members resist tasks
- team members keep asking for your advice and help
- worrying comments from others (e.g. customers, your boss or other people in the organisation)
- team members question their role, or worry excessively about their competence
- team members leave – or worse, ask for more money!

This is by no means an exhaustive list and it is important to be sensitive to signs that things are not going well. Also, these problems may well occur from time to time anyway: what matters is *how often they arise* and *how long they stay*.

> **Summary:** *Techniques for effective delegation*
>
> Effective delegation is based on a number of simple, common-sense principles that provide the keys to successful management. These include:
>
> - If you give people authority they will take responsibility.
> - The people closest to the action (meaning the task, customer or front-line) know best.
> - If you treat people like robots they will behave like robots.
>
> The process for effective delegation remains the same at any level. Having first built up trust the leader needs to be clear about what to delegate; match person to task; communicate clearly and agree objectives; provide sufficient resources; monitor progress, and review and assess overall performance.
>
> Effective delegators should:
>
> - Challenge team members to find their own solutions.
> - Encourage creativity, innovation and initiative.
> - Empower their team so they don't just take responsibility for a task, but for their whole job, constantly making positive improvements.
> - Set clear, challenging objectives.
> - Agree and regularly monitor performance measures.
> - Prevent conflicts arising in the long term.
> - Recognise and deal with conflicts that have arisen.
> - Lead your team and give them a framework that brings out their talents and skills.

Further information

Successful Delegation in a Week
J. Kourdi, Hodder Headline, 1999

Delegation Skills
B. Tepper, Irwin, 1994

Delegating Authority
A. Schwarz, Cassell, 1995

Empowering People
A.M. Stewart, FT/Pitman, 1994

Developing yourself and your staff

Introduction

The most valuable and influential resource in any organisation is its people: and often it is the most expensive too. The leader therefore needs to nurture and develop the skills of both the team and the individual to face ongoing challenges and to deliver success. Furthermore, individuals' talents and skills can often be hidden (even from the individual!) and the leader needs to challenge and support people in order to achieve their full potential. This process has to start with the leader, both to set an example but also to ensure that they are up to the task. This process of staff development, therefore, has several stages:

1. It should start with the *leader's own development needs*, ensuring that you possess all of the skills needed to lead the team.
2. The next step is *analysing training needs*. The support of personnel and training experts is invaluable, but ultimately it is the leader that knows (or should know) the needs of the tasks, team and each individual, and it is the leader that needs to support each person.
3. *Delivering* the most appropriate and effective training.
4. *Relating the training to the tasks that need to be completed* – and ensuring that the organisation and individual derive maximum benefit – is often overlooked, yet this work-based aspect is fundamental in determining whether the development activity provides lasting benefit or not.
5. *Monitoring and evaluating* the team and individuals is the final part of the process for the leader, and this is usually accomplished through appraisals, mentoring and work planning discussions (e.g. delegation). It therefore takes the leader straight back to stage 1 and the cycle continues.

Types of development activity

One of the biggest dangers a leader can make is to assume that there are one or two – or half a dozen – methods for learning; there are in fact many more and some of the most popular are listed below. Choosing the type of development that is most appropriate often depends on:

- cost
- time available for development
- the type of individual and their particular learning style
- the immediate needs of the task and of the job role
- the longer-term needs of the job role.

Type of activity	Benefits	Disadvantages
1. **External short courses (normally between 1 and 5 days)**	• Intensive • Expert tuition	• Expensive • Can be difficult to relate to the work environment • Duration and timing
2. **In-house training**	• Tailored	• Expensive • Potential personality clashes
3. **Job shadowing**	• Relevant and work-based • Low cost	• Picks up bad practices • Does not generate innovation
4. **Distance learning**	• Learn at a pace and place that is most convenient	• Requires self-discipline • Can be isolated
5. **Qualification programmes (e.g. NVQs, Certificates, Diplomas, Degrees)**	• Thorough and rigorous • Meet specified, recognised standards • Encourages the individual	• Time-consuming • Expensive • Not necessarily relevant or practical
6. **Reading**	• Inexpensive • Tailored	• No feedback
7. **Software packages**	• Consistent method • Can be interactive • Useful for technical skills	• Expensive • Frustrating if there is no feedback
8. **Research projects**	• Self-directed • Work-based	• Need self-discipline • Need specific skills of research
9. **Outward bound courses**	• Team-building • Confidence-building	• Can be uncomfortable (in several ways!) • Expensive

DEVELOPING YOURSELF AND YOUR STAFF

Type of activity	Benefits	Disadvantages
10. Role playing	• Inexpensive • Focused • Share experiences	• Can be uncomfortable • Success largely depends on the quality of feedback
11. Workshops	• Can mix internal perspectives with external views • Practical	• Can be easily dominated by others
12. Learning from other people's experience	• Good learning opportunities across a broad range	• Can be subjective and broad
13. Day release/ Night classes	• Interaction with others • Clear focus on the topic	• Expensive • Timing can cause problems – not always feasible
14. Learning from mistakes	• Memorable • Character-forming	• Mistakes can be costly • Requires a positive attitude in the face of adversity
15. The Internet	• Scope of subjects, ideas and experiences • Inexpensive	• Not work-based • Can be difficult to find what you want
16. Customer complaints	• Clear and immediate • Entirely work-based	• Demotivating • Learning is secondary to resolving the issue
17. Videos/Audios	• Convenient • Wide-ranging subjects	• Quality is variable • Can be difficult to implement and relate to work
18. Life experiences	• Rich in examples of best and worst practice, and ideas	• Not always relevant to work – need sifting!
19. Mentoring and coaching	• Tailored and focused on the individual's needs • Regular • Clear direction and feedback	• Success depends on the quality and strength of the relationship

Type of activity	Benefits	Disadvantages
20. **Apprenticeship**	• Achieves high standards	• Largely suited to learning technical skills • Can be expensive and time-consuming
21. **Secondment**	• Broad perspective • Motivational • Focused	• Time-consuming • Learning curves may hamper effectiveness
22. **Team work**	• Learn from others • Supportive	• Success depends on the quality and abilities of the team

Table 4 Advantages and disadvantages of different types of development activity

Investors in People (IIP)

Investors in People (IIP) was established by the UK government to encourage employers to actively encourage employers to develop their workforce and improve business performance. The programme provides a useful framework for anyone wishing to improve staff skills and unlock the full potential of their employees.

Structure of IIP

IIP is a UK national standard, and to achieve it employers have to:

1. Make a formal commitment to the training and development of their employees, and
2. Develop and implement an action plan for companies to follow that is linked to the company's objectives.

The IIP programme is supported and implemented in the UK by Training and Enterprise Councils (TECs) (or Local Enterprise Councils (LECs) in Scotland). They assist companies in setting up the programme, and they also conduct a full assessment of the company at an agreed time, leading to the final award.

A company that attains IIP has demonstrated that it is:

- Committed to staff development.
- Training and development needs are regularly reviewed.
- Specific action is taken to develop individuals.
- The process is regularly reviewed and improved.

The four principles of IIP are:

DEVELOPING YOURSELF AND YOUR STAFF

1. *Commitment* – a commitment from the senior managers right through the organisation to train and develop new and existing employees.
2. *Planning* – a plan from the organisation detailing *how* it will routinely include training into its business plan. This includes linking employees' training to the business's objectives and setting targets for training.
3. *Action* – evidence of how the organisation has delivered on its plan: how staff training has been completed to meet the organisation's objectives, and how development needs are being *continuously* assessed and met.
4. *Evaluation* – assessing the effectiveness of training activities is the final phase of IIP. It involves assessing the original plan against what is actually happening, and also assessing the quality of the training that is being provided and the benefits that result.

Implementing IIP

The following process outlines the actions that are required to attain IIP:

1. In the UK, *contact your local TEC or LEC* and ask for the tool-kit that explains how to get started and what to do.
2. *Appoint a programme champion* responsible for managing and overseeing the IIP programme.
3. *Undertake a self-assessment* of current training and development activities in the organisation; in particular, consider:

    - how well-trained staff are *at all levels*;
    - how you decide to train people – the criteria and process that is used;
    - the methods used to train and develop people;
    - the overall priority that training is given and the resources that are used.

4. *Produce a written plan*, ideally derived from the overall business plan, that details:

    - the process for assessing and agreeing training needs;
    - how employees will be trained and developed within their organisation;
    - the resources, including finance, that will be available.

5. *Implementing IIP* is the next, and perhaps most crucial, stage. The advantage of IIP is that it is entirely flexible in how it is implemented: each organisation produces its own training programme and ongoing development process to suit its specific needs, and then takes action to achieve this.
6. *To attain the IIP standard a portfolio is produced* which is assessed by the

ONE STOP LEADERSHIP

local TEC or LEC. This should contain the business plan and written evidence showing how IIP has been implemented.

Finally, experience has shown that there are several major benefits of IIP including:

- improving employee performance;
- enhancing motivation and morale;
- retaining and recruiting high-quality staff;
- improving and enhancing the reputation of the organisation;
- increasing competitiveness and company profits overall.

Summary: *Personal development planning*

Continuous Professional Development (CPD) is essential for a leader to stay fully in control and effective in a constantly changing business world. Many professional organisations (e.g. engineers, lawyers and accountants) now require their members to fulfil a minimum level of CPD activities each year, and to keep a log of these activities.

The self-development cycle

It is important for leaders to consider the whole of the development cycle, both for their own development and their team's. The seven stages of the cycle are:

1. *Establish the purpose* – the leader needs to keep the overall aim firmly in mind, and then ensure that all activities *directly support* this aim. Without this clear goal in mind it is often difficult to stay on track, keep momentum or maintain motivation.
2. *Identify development needs* – the development needs must be identified and a programme for meeting those needs should be devised. In particular, the needs must be realistic and time-constrained, with a definite deadline.
3. *Look at development opportunities* – deciding how to meet the development needs is the next stage, and this may include a mix of formal and informal methods. As well as effectiveness, cost and timing, bear in mind your own preferred learning style: what approach suits you (or your team member) best?

4. *Formulate an action plan* – this will be necessary for more complex development needs requiring a range of activities or an ongoing process. You should also consider how the development process will be *supported,* perhaps by a mentor within the organisation.
5. *Undertake development* – this is the central part of the whole process. It is worth considering specifically how the results will be integrated into workplace activities.
6. *Record outcomes* – keep track of development activities in order to:

    – Assess results against planned objectives.
    – Review progress and understand what methods work best.
    – Plan future activities.

7. *Review and evaluate* – the process of recording and evaluating is often completed using a *Personal Development Log,* and evaluating the event will help to assess whether the original objective has been met and the development need fulfilled. You should evaluate:

    – The development activity: whether it met your needs and was useful.
    – The knowledge, skills and understanding you gained: what you can now do.
    – How the activity will make a difference in the workplace.
    – The next steps: for example the activity might have highlighted further areas for development or additional tasks that can be completed.

The success of the personal development cycle depends on repeating the planning process regularly (at least every year, preferably every six months or when circumstances change, such as taking on a new role).

Further information

Industrial Society, 48 Bryanston Square, London W1H 7LN

Training Enterprise and Education Directorate and Employment Department, Moorfoot, Sheffield, S1 4PQ

One Stop Personnel
D. Martin, ICSA Publishing, 1999

Introducing Investors in People
M. McLuskey, Kogan Page, 1996

Managing Change through Training and Development
J. Stewart, Kogan Page, 1996

Ready Made Activities for Developing Your Staff
D. Taylor and S. Bishop, FT/Pitman, 1995

Financial leadership and building shareholder value

Introduction

One of the fundamental responsibilities of the leader in a modern commercial enterprise is to increase the long-term value of a business. A key technique for achieving this is using *Shareholder Value Analysis (SVA)*. This is essentially a finance-based strategic management approach, which has gained rapid and significant popularity in recent years.

It is based on the view that standard methods for calculating the financial value of an undertaking are often too short-term or retrospective (i.e. favouring an historical perspective). This belief started in the USA and has since spread world-wide as businesses become ever more global and complex, and also as a result of a steady rise in mergers and acquisitions. In this rapidly evolving commercial environment business decisions that are based on traditional accounting techniques, such as price/earnings ratios or growth in profits, have proved to be increasingly inadequate. This is because it is possible to make business decisions which improve these traditional measures and ratios in the short term (i.e. reducing expenditure on research or developing people), but whose effect will be to reduce the long-term success and profitability of the business – and the wealth of the shareholders. Therefore, the basic belief underlying shareholder value is that a business only adds value for its shareholders when equity returns exceed equity costs.

Shareholder Value Analysis (SVA) is the popular antidote to this short-term bias, and is entirely concerned with controlling and managing profits flows *over a long-term perspective*. Features of SVA are that it:

- Does not emphasise accounting standards for financial management, preferring instead a more practical, context-sensitive approach that is better suited to each separate business.
- Takes into account commercial risk and discounting future cash flows (i.e. taking into account the time value of money) when making commercial (and particularly investment) decisions. With SVA, financial considerations and techniques are much more to the

fore when managers are making commercial decisions: issues such as return, risk, cash flow and value routinely guide managers in their operational as well as their strategic decisions.
- Requires comprehensive commercial information across a range of factors compared to more traditional measures.

Checklist – applying shareholder value analysis

There are several techniques that underpin shareholder value analysis, although many reputable consultancies also provide expert advice and guidance on how to enhance financial performance *over the long term*. This may be particularly welcome as shareholder value is a complex subject with financial and general commercial aspects needing to be understood and applied.

Calculating shareholder value (i.e. the value of the business or how successfully it is performing)

Calculating shareholder value is based on the following formula:

$$\text{Shareholder value} = \frac{\text{Future cash flows (those generated during the planning period plus residual values)}}{\text{Weighted average cost of capital (WACC)}}$$

Definitions

- *Future cash flows* – these are determined by growth, returns and risk. Each of these factors is influenced by seven key *value drivers* which must be managed in order to maximise shareholder value:
    - sales growth (or turnover growth)
    - cash profit margin
    - cash tax rate
    - working capital available to grow the business
    - capital expenditure (or fixed capital)
    - the period of competitive advantage (some people prefer instead to focus on the planning period)
    - the weighted average cost of capital (WACC), adjusted for risk and inflation.
- *Residual value* includes cash flows generated *after* the planning period (normally three to five years).
- *Weighted Average Cost of Capital (WACC)* is the cost of equity added to the cost of debt. The value of the concept of WACC is as an expression of the return that a company must earn to justify the cash and investment that it uses. The WACC therefore expresses the opportunity cost of the

assets in use. WACC is also entirely market-driven: if the assets cannot earn the required return, then investors will withdraw their funds from the business.

Top management commitment

For SVA to become firmly established and succeed, senior managers need to accept that creating and maximising the *value* of the business, in the long term as well as short, is the overriding commercial objective. This often requires an acceptance that traditional measures and approaches fall short of achieving this objective.

Understanding the *value drivers* of the business and setting clear objectives

Realising shareholder value is about maximising cash flows, and to achieve this the key value drivers of the business need to be clearly recognised. These are the seven value drivers listed above. The impact of how value drivers can relate to each other is highlighted by the example of improvements in the cash profit margin being affected by sales and expenses, which are in turn driven by a number of other factors such as customer-base, pricing, purchasing costs, sales expenses, etc. These are in turn each affected by other influences, and so on across the business.

The key, therefore, is to understand *how* the factors affecting the financial performance of the business interrelate, and then focus on the key drivers of improved performance. This approach links financial and operational objectives and results in a framework for:

- setting performance targets (i.e. increasing revenue per customer) for individuals and teams;
- reviewing the business's financial success;
- benchmarking the strength of the business against competitors;
- developing and implementing strategic plans.

It is a difficult process to identify the key factors influencing each value driver, and invariably involves trial and error. However, this process is fundamental to managing, controlling and improving the business so that its financial performance is enhanced.

Communicating the new approach

The technical financial aspects of SVA can deter many managers and individuals, and it is often more effective simply to communicate the broad nature of creating shareholder value, particularly when considering future plans, direction and strategy, or when appraising potential projects.

Perhaps more importantly, managers need to understand the significance of identifying, controlling and improving the performance of the value drivers – and the key factors influencing them. Adopting SVA and setting new targets should challenge teams and individuals, and as a result may encounter resistance. Previous approaches will need to be re-evaluated and possibly discarded in favour of new targets.

Training staff

SVA is best viewed as a change process requiring line managers to be fully trained, flexible and supportive. An important first step in implementing SVA is for managers to be introduced to the value drivers: what they are, why they are important and how they can be influenced. As with any change process early, high-profile successes help to establish the new approach, highlighting the benefits and winning over sceptics.

Align the business's information systems so that they effectively monitor progress

In order to build financial performance proactively and unlock shareholder value, senior managers need to be able to measure and monitor information concerning the key value drivers and targets that have been set. This will help to provide a picture of the overall effect that this action is having on performance. However, this may require new reports and systems, and the infrastructure will almost certainly need to be adapted to take account of these new and different requirements.

Review employees' remuneration schemes

An approach that values SVA should emphasise the importance of increasing shareholder value over *time*, rather than focusing on short-term profit growth alone (which could be achieved at the expense of the long-term prospects of the business). In addition, individuals' incentives and bonuses need to reflect success in controlling the value drivers that they control and meeting agreed objectives.

Regularly review progress and targets

An approach that emphasises long-term value creation will take time to establish. Key steps to achieving this include:

- Communicating the approach, in particular, what it means for the business and the individual.
- Training and supporting individuals so that they can manage the value drivers that they control.

- Setting clear, realistic targets that are attainable, challenging and will improve the financial standing of the business.
- Implementing appropriate incentive schemes.
- Measuring and monitoring progress.

Failing to emphasise value creation can often result in managers focusing on targets which are no longer relevant, or which are actually harmful to the long-term value of the business.

Summary: *Benefits and potential pitfalls of Shareholder Value Analysis*

There are a number of key issues for the leader to consider when implementing shareholder value analysis:

- How well accepted is the concept; does it fit with company culture, and do you have the support and understanding of senior colleagues?
- Would you and your colleagues leading SVA benefit from the advice and guidance of experienced professional advisers in this area?
- Are the targets for increasing shareholder value SMART (Specific, Measurable, Achievable, Realistic/Relevant, and Time-constrained)?
- Do the business's shareholders understand and approve of the new approach that is being adopted in their name?

Benefits

SVA provides three main business benefits:

- a long-term financial view on which to form strategic and operational decisions;
- a flexible and universal approach that is suited to different businesses, accounting conventions and commercial requirements;
- SVA forces the leader to focus the business on future revenues, profitability and hence customers. This is in contrast to other traditional measures that tend to be cost-based, bearing little relation to the economic income generated during a period.

Potential pitfalls

Problems can arise chiefly with the *execution* of value analysis. The key difficulties include:

- Estimating future cash flows. This is a key component of shareholder value analysis and can be extremely difficult to complete accurately, leading to incorrect figures forming the basis for strategic decisions.
- A long and complex process for developing and implementing a system for SVA.
- Communicating the approach to managers and gaining commitment.
- Obtaining the right information. Managing shareholder value generally requires much more complete information than traditional measures.

Further information

In Search of Shareholder Value – Managing the Drivers of Performance
A. Black, P. Wright, J. Bachman, J. Davies, Financial Times, 1998

Creating Shareholder Value – The new standard for business performance
A. Rappaport, The Free Press, 1986

Corporate Strategy and Finance Decisions
A.N. Grundy, Kogan Page, 1992

Strategic Financial Decisions – A guide to the evaluation and monitoring of business strategy
D. Allen, CIMA/Kogan Page, 1994

Handling conflict

> **Introduction**
>
> In any team or work situation conflicts may arise: this can often happen when work is delegated, even when there has been careful preparation in advance, and also during times of change, uncertainty or stress. There are many possible causes of conflict including *personal clashes* resulting from an argument; a poor relationship or basic personality clash; or a personality defect such as bullying. There are also *professional causes* of conflict. These might arise from different approaches and ways of working; a fear of change; concern or dissatisfaction with some aspect of employment, or office rumours.

Preventing conflict

There are a number of practical ways of preventing conflict arising, and in this case prevention is certainly better than cure as conflicts at work can be particularly difficult to recover from and require a great deal of time and effort.

The first step in preventing conflict is for the leader to ensure regular communication. By maintaining a dialogue the leader will be able to spot conflicts and resentments building up. It will also help in other areas, for example deciding how, when and to whom to delegate; who to promote; and where further staff training and development is required.

In preventing conflict it is important for the leader to assess the culture and management style of the organisation. Is it too aggressive? Is there an atmosphere of intense competition, rivalry or blame? Is it conservative, hierarchical and not open to discussion? The leader (who may, for example, be a supervisor or team leader) may not be able to change the culture of the business, but a clear understanding makes it possible to make allowances and build the best team that suits the required goals. Encouraging teamwork and building team spirit is therefore a vital element in preventing conflict or ill-will, and if the leader can instil a sense of common purpose this will certainly reduce the likelihood of conflict. Encouraging teamwork will also ensure that people are used to working together and increase understanding.

Other elements in preventing conflict include setting clear, formal, professional standards – making people aware of what is acceptable behaviour and what is not. This can be accomplished in a wide variety of ways, starting from the interview process and including the example that the leader sets, their way of working, treating people and approaching business situations. The leadership style, therefore, needs to fit with the tasks to be accomplished and the team that is being led. Clear, open communication and an open door policy are generally regarded as the best approaches for a leader wishing to promote an effective, harmonious team. If people feel that they can discuss a particular situation then the leader is much more likely to be able to defuse any problems that may be developing.

Case study: *The dangers of weak leadership during a time of conflict*

Two company directors had an intense dislike of each other: they struggled to be civil to each other in public, but often failed. Their mutual dislike was at times completely irrational from two individuals who were in all other respects talented and professional. The truth was that they simply could not understand or agree, reacting almost instinctively against anything that the other said. (The animosity was well known within the small business, which employed 30 staff and had a turnover of £4 million a year.)

The conflict was contained as far as possible by the Chairman and his Finance Director/Company Secretary, who often acted as conciliators between the two. Indeed, the two arguing directors often sought to gain their support in their battles to outwit the other! This comic situation had a number of curious and damaging side-effects: effectively the company was split into two camps and this was reinforced by the two directions taken by the business. Ultimately, and perhaps inevitably, disaster struck: sales fell and cash started drying up. The Chairman and Finance Director were busy fire-fighting external problems rescheduling suppliers' debts, trying to find potential investors and struggling to keep the support of the bank. Eventually the company went into receivership and ceased trading.

Clearly the final outcome could have happened anyway, but the situation of the two arguing directors

> was an unwelcome distraction during the good times – and a dangerous drain on resources during bad. The failing was one of weak leadership from the Chairman and other Board members, who were totally unaccustomed to this kind of open warfare. The bottom line was that the conflict had to be resolved quickly: either the directors had to work together or one (or both) had to go. This was not apparent at the time, largely because each of the individuals was so talented and capable in their own right, but in truth their talent was utterly negated by their bitter antipathy.

Resolving conflict

Resolving conflict is one of the most difficult, stressful and important aspects of successful leadership. If the conflict is personal it is usually best to avoid getting too involved: the leader's role is to limit the effects on the organisation and make it clear to the parties involved that there is a job that needs to be done. Frequently, leaders – even experienced ones – fall into the trap of thinking that management is about making friends! This can happen in particular because conflicts arise infrequently, or suddenly, or both. It is also important to remember not to underestimate conflicts: they can be very serious matters to the parties involved, however minor they may appear to the leader. It is also important that they take time to think carefully about the situation before acting: it is easy for the leader to undermine their own position, and perhaps even inflame the conflict, by making the wrong move at the wrong time. The leader's role might therefore be to think about how best to restore fairness or common sense to the situation, meeting the needs of the task, the team as a whole and the individuals involved.

When conflict arises there are a number of approaches that the leader can adopt. The best approach depends on the type and nature of the dispute; the task, team and individuals involved, and the background environment (for example, whether it is a regular conflict, or whether it is prompted by external factors). There is no single way of resolving conflicts, although there are some common-sense approaches and tactics that are widely used by successful leaders:

1. *Talk to each person individually.* The leader should generally try to remain neutral, objective and constructive; it is vital to remain in control and confident. Letting each person express their grievances is a valuable means of getting the people involved to see the situation clearly, away

from the emotion and stress that conflict usually brings. Listening and reflecting back the key issues can also help the people involved to deal with the problem, perhaps by encouraging them to explore possible solutions themselves, or else deciding the best course of action yourself.

2. *Make the parties to the conflict face their situation and communicate.* A danger is for the leader to get too involved in the detail and complexity of the conflict, to the point that their authority and ability to resolve it is completely undermined. The parties to the conflict need to understand that they created it, it is their responsibility and they need to help resolve it: clear, regular, open communication is a good first step.

3. *Consider making them work together.* It may be that the problem could be resolved if each person understood the other, and their situation, better. It may also be that there is no other alternative: they will have to get on so get them to realise the fact and start as they may mean to go on!

4. *Remove the problem.* If the difficulty is influenced or exacerbated by an outside cause then the best approach the leader can take is to consider what action can be taken to remove or alleviate the problem.

> **Summary:** *Preventing and managing conflict*
>
> Implementing routine measures, such as regular team briefings, appraisals or simply maintaining an open and blame-free environment, is important in preventing conflicts arising. It is also worth giving some thought to how you might pre-empt conflict arising from specific situations, and how you will react if problems occur.
>
> However, if difficulties do arise (and at some stage they almost certainly will for *any* leader) then there are a number of important points to remember:
>
> - *Communicate with your peers.* You are probably not alone, and however bitter the dispute has become – or threatens to become – there should be people around you who can act as a sounding board, and with whom you can discuss the situation. (This usually needs to be done in the strictest confidence.) It might even be possible that there are other people who can help you to reduce or remove the problem, and alleviate the dispute.
> - *Be decisive.* Do not simply hope that the difficulty will go away: take charge early, decide what outcome you want and then set out to achieve it.

This might mean no more than setting a time limit and waiting for the dispute to 'blow over' or solve itself, or it could mean getting much more involved and mediating. The extent of the leader's intervention depends on the complexity of the dispute and the depth of feeling involved. However, most disputes can usually be reduced to one or two key points that cause deadlock and animosity: break those quickly and amicably and the dispute could well disappear.

- *Consider all of the implications of the conflict – and its solution.* As a leader you should understand the full implications of the dispute – *who* is affected and *what* is affected – both by the problem and its solution. For example, will the outcome set an undesirable precedent? What signal will it give to others? Remember to consider the longer-term picture when resolving disputes, or you may just be storing up problems for the future.
- *Take time to gather and consider the facts.* Before deciding what action to take you should make sure that you understand the facts, and remember that the more heated and acrimonious the dispute is the more the truth can be distorted! Your approach and actions should always be based on the *reality* of the situation and what you know to be true – focusing on the needs of the *task, team* and *individual* – rather than hearsay or speculation.
- *Avoid becoming emotional or losing objectivity.* It can be easy to get drawn into a conflict or manipulated into taking sides. You should be aware of the pitfalls and decide early on how you will approach the dispute.

Above all, when handling conflict you should remember that you are dealing with people, and you need to be sure that you respect individuals' views and feelings. If you do not you could find that, although resolved, the conflict is only the first in a long line, born of mistrust and resentment. Effective communications and influencing skills are therefore essential in resolving conflict (see COMMUNICATION SKILLS).

Further information

Tough Talking: How to handle awkward situations
D. Martin, FT/Pitman, 1996

Manipulating Meetings
D. Martin, FT/Pitman, 1996

Successful Assertiveness in a Week
D. Michelli, Hodder Headline, 1994

Knowledge management

Introduction

Managing knowledge means no more than applying and using information for a practical purpose. Management knowledge is also, perhaps more scientifically, termed *intellectual capital*. Increasingly, organisations are recognising the benefits of using all their employees' skills and knowledge, as a result of a number of factors including:

- Increasing competitive pressures.
- The rapid development of 'high-tech' industries such as biotechnology, software and services, where success relies largely on the knowledge and expertise of people.
- The fact that the value of the intellectual property in many products (from pharmaceuticals to computer software) is much greater than the physical content or labour.

Benefits of managing knowledge

Increasingly leaders need to manage knowledge in order to:

- *Ensure that costly mistakes are avoided (and are certainly not repeated)* – where knowledge of past events is recorded, this experience can be used to understand why decisions were made and avoid repeating the failures of the past.
- *Achieve faster response times* – increased flexibility and speed to market can result by combining knowledge in interdisciplinary teams.
- *Improve products and services* – by monitoring factors such as product failures and customer views, quality improvements can be achieved.
- *Improve customer service* – identifying and disseminating information about best practices will contribute to improvements in customer service.
- *Increase revenues and the financial value of the organisation* – intellectual property, including patents and copyright, has grown enormously as an income source (and, for listed companies, a driver of share prices).

Techniques for effectively managing knowledge

There are five key aspects to managing knowledge:
1. mapping (or auditing) the existing knowledge-base
2. increasing organisational knowledge
3. maintaining knowledge
4. exploiting knowledge
5. protecting knowledge.

Mapping the existing knowledge-base

Because knowledge is often overlooked, neglected or confined to one person (or a handful of people) it can often be difficult to assess. The knowledge audit should therefore:

- *Define* what knowledge assets exist in the organisation, i.e. what information or intellectual property is there that would be difficult or expensive to replace.
- *Locate* those knowledge assets and who keeps (or 'owns') them.
- *Classify* the knowledge assets and see how they relate to other assets. It may be that the answer to one problem lies elsewhere in the organisation, unrecognised!

Increasing organisational knowledge

Once the organisation has effectively audited its stock of intellectual capital, it needs to match what it has with what the strategy or business plan says is needed. The leader's task is then to increase the knowledge-base so that the organisation can achieve its aims. Essentially, there are three methods of adding to the knowledge-base:

1. *Buying knowledge* by hiring staff with the necessary skills; forming alliances and partnerships with other organisations, or outsourcing functions to organisations where the required expertise already exists.
2. *Renting knowledge* by hiring consultants or subcontracting work.
3. *Developing knowledge* by training and developing people, and also creating opportunities and processes within the organisation to support continuous learning.

Maintaining knowledge and avoid 'knowledge gaps'

Widespread redundancies and 'downsizing' programmes in the 1990s eventually highlighted the dangers of removing people with expertise and experience. Organisations found that they had lost a great deal of valuable knowledge, experience and skills that they had not taken into account, and this had significant implications in areas like decision-making, problem-solving, innovation and management generally. To avoid knowledge gaps leaders should consider:

- Redeploying managers, rather than making them redundant.
- Developing managers as trainers so that they can pass on their skills.
- Using managers as mentors so that they can pass on their experience.
- Ensuring that notice periods are adequate for staff with key skills, so that there is time for these to be captured and ideally passed on.
- Ensuring adequate succession planning so that when people leave or retire their skills and experience can be passed on.
- Maintaining networks with people externally that possess the necessary skills – possibly developing a network of suppliers or consultants.

The leader needs to strike a balance between leaving the knowledge worker to continue with their work, and ensuring that the person's skills and experience are developed and maintained. There needs to be a balance between trust and control, and the best way to achieve this is often simply to establish an understanding and rapport with the knowledge worker.

Exploiting knowledge

Often the leader does not realise the value of the knowledge that is before them. Typically, knowledge can be used in two ways:

1. *Internally*, to improve the organisation's success and effectiveness, and
2. *Externally* for commercial advantage.

> **Case study:** *Auditing intellectual capital*
>
> Following an audit one approach might be to circulate a list of the resources available to the heads of each department or function. Technology and intranets can also play a useful role in disseminating information. Another, complementary approach could be to inform managers and mentors. Whatever approach is taken the goal has to be to cascade information throughout the organisation, and ensure that the knowledge is exploited internally. There is one famous story of a drug company that spent many years and millions of dollars developing a new drug, only to find that the patent had already been taken – *by another part of the same company*!

Leaders should also be alive to the commercial potential of their intellectual property. People are used to selling products and are generally less used to selling *people*, yet this may be a major commercial opportunity. Selling people's expertise not only generates revenue but also raises profile – highlighting the fact that your organisation has significant skills and experience. In my experience finance managers and company secretaries are often the people most alive to the commercial opportunities of exploiting information.

Protecting knowledge

Knowledge falls into two categories:

1. *Explicit knowledge* such as patents, copyright or information codified in handbooks, recipes or procedures.
2. *Tacit knowledge*, which is retained by individuals and includes learning, experience, observation, deduction and informally acquired knowledge.

The leader should ensure that both types of knowledge are nurtured and protected. Explicit knowledge can be protected through legal procedures (e.g. patents) and, if necessary, legal action. Although tacit knowledge can also be protected by legal means, such as non-compete clauses in employment contracts, this is usually less satisfactory. A more realistic approach is simply to ensure that the relevant knowledge is retained and passed on.

Summary: *Managing knowledge*

Schemes that map organisational knowledge provide leaders with several important benefits:

1. They outline the existing knowledge level and resources within the organisation.
2. They can track knowledge and skills that are not currently used but may be of value to the organisation later.
3. They save money by using existing in-house expertise.
4. They influence strategy and future plans, helping to decide which direction an organisation can take.
5. They highlight strengths and weaknesses within the organisation.

Further information

Managing Knowledge
D. Wilson, Butterworth-Heinemann, 1996

Transformational Learning: Renewing your company through knowledge and skills
D. Tobin, John Wiley, 1996

Intellectual Capital
A. Brooking, ITP, 1996

Wellsprings of Knowledge: Building and sustaining the sources of innovation
D. Leonard-Barton, Harvard Business School Press, 1995

The Knowledge Creating Company: How Japanese companies create the dynamics of innovation
I. Nonaka and H. Takeuchi, Oxford University Press, 1995

Leadership skills

Introduction

There is a wide range of views on the skills required for effective leadership. To some leadership is synonymous with management, whereas for others leading is more simply about *getting the best from people* – managing people so that they work together to move in the direction that the leader sets. The logical extension of this view is that leadership is a transferable skill, it can be taught, and this belief has gained enormously in popularity over the last thirty years, promoted by a wealth of leadership writers such as John Adair and Warren Bennis. By contrast, the 'Great Man' theories of leadership, which previously predominated, are now seen as increasingly irrelevant to the fast-moving, complex and much less hierarchical world that has developed.

Action-centred leadership

One of the most famous, enduring and useful views on leadership is John Adair's *Action-Centred Leadership* model. Adair defines leadership in terms of three overlapping and interdependent circles – task, team and individual – and his approach emphasises these three areas as forming the boundaries for what the leader must do to be effective.

Task, team and individual

Adair's concept asserts that these three *needs* are central to the task of leadership, as people expect their leaders to help them achieve the common task; build the synergy of teamwork, and respond to individuals' needs.

- The *task* needs work groups or organisations to come into effect because one person alone cannot accomplish it.
- The *team* needs constant promotion and group cohesiveness to ensure that it functions efficiently. The team functions on the 'united we stand, divided we fall' principle.
- The *individual's* needs are the physical – salary; and the psychological – recognition; sense of purpose and achievement; status; and the need to give and receive from others in a work environment.

For Adair, the task, team and individual needs overlap as follows:

- *Achieving the task* builds the team and satisfies the individuals.
- *If the team needs are not met,* the team lacks cohesiveness and performance on the task is impaired and individual satisfaction is reduced.
- *If individual needs are not met,* the team will lack cohesiveness and performance of the task will be impaired.

Adair's view is that leadership exists at three different levels: *team leadership* of teams of 5–20 people; *operational leadership*, where a number of team leaders report to one leader, and *strategic leadership* of a whole business or organisation, with overall accountability for all levels of leadership. At whatever level leadership is being exercised Adair's model takes the view that task, team and individual needs must be constantly considered. The strengths of the concept are that it is timeless and is not culture- or situation-dependent. Another strength of the concept is that it can help the leader to identify where they may be operating out of kilter with the real needs of the group or situation.

Leadership tasks

In order to fulfil the three aspects of leadership (task, team and individual) and achieve success there are eight functions that must be performed and developed by the leader.

1. *Defining the task* – the leader needs to ensure that the task is distilled into a clear objective that is SMART (Specific, Measurable, Assignable, Realistic/Relevant and Time-constrained).
2. *Planning* – this requires a search for alternatives, and is best done with others in an open-minded, positive and creative way. Contingencies should be planned for and plans should be tested.
3. *Briefing* – team briefing is a basic leadership function that is essential in order to create the right conditions, promote teamwork and motivate each individual.
4. *Controlling* – leadership is frequently about getting maximum results with the minimum of resources. To achieve this leaders need self-control, have good control systems in place and be able to delegate and monitor others effectively.
5. *Evaluating* – this function of leadership requires leaders to be good at assessing the consequences of actions; evaluating team performance; appraising and training individuals, and judging people.
6. *Motivating* – a central task of the leader is to motivate others. There are six main principles when motivating others. These are: be motivated yourself; select people who are highly motivated; set realistic and challenging targets; remember that progress motivates; provide fair rewards, and give recognition.

7. *Organising* – this function of leadership requires good leaders to organise *themselves*, their *team* and the *organisation* (including its structures and processes). Leading change requires a clear purpose and effective organisation to achieve results.
8. *Setting an example* – leaders need to set an example to individuals and the team: a bad example is noticed more than a good one, and setting an example is, therefore, something that must be worked at constantly.

These leadership functions need to be constantly developed and honed so that the leader's success is improved. In that way leadership is itself a process of continuous development, education and improvement.

Checklist – ensuring effective leadership

Effective leadership has many advantages: it is the way that people are led through changing or difficult times; it helps to spread common understanding and a sense of purpose; it generates enthusiasm, teamwork and motivation, and consistently gets the best from people. Effective, consistent leadership relies on the following factors:

Avoiding the pitfalls of poor leadership

There are several dangers that can arise around leaders, often quite unwittingly. These include the danger that leaders can stifle innovation, possibly even reducing confidence, by being too overbearing. There is a danger that leadership can exert too great a pull on people, not necessarily as a result of the leader's actions but perhaps resulting from other external factors. Leadership can also lead to the cult of personality where the leader is revered, usually to the detriment of the leader, the people they are leading and the task they are trying to accomplish. The final danger is that leaders who are too tough, ruthless or 'macho' will conflict with others, usually their peers, and split teams and the organisation.

Empowering leadership

Often leaders, particularly inexperienced ones, believe that charisma is the defining skill of leadership and brandish it, more or less effectively, all of the time. The problem here is that charisma is frequently ineffective or inappropriate: it may dominate people and create a reliance on the leader, instead of fostering initiative. Developing an involved, committed and ultimately successful workforce requires empowering leadership, the key attributes of which are:

- a belief in constant learning rather than assumed mastery;
- the development of high self-esteem in others;

- a willingness to ask questions, admit weaknesses and listen to answers;
- strong interpersonal skills, including an appreciation of other people and sensitivity to individuals;
- an ability to engender trust, build relationships and inspire others; and the capacity to trust others;
- the ability and desire to develop leadership in others;
- the capacity to handle criticism by listening and drawing out people's concerns;
- a capacity to develop an effective vision of the future;
- an approach that possesses, values and nurtures innovation and initiative;
- the ability to communicate well at every level;
- integrity and trustworthiness;
- mentoring, coaching and counselling skills.

Be clear and focused on what you want to achieve

It is important to understand that leadership is a dynamic process and relies on the leader creating a vision and gaining people's commitment for that ideal. There are few certainties with leadership and to that extent it differs considerably from management, which tends to emphasise the more routine *administration* of a specific function. The leader therefore needs to be clear about their goals.

Understand present realities

It is easy for the leader to focus on a distant, utopian vision – a dream – and ignore the immediate obstacles. Quite often these start with the leader, and initially many leaders may not feel comfortable with the role and may lack the confidence, authority or respect that is vital for success. In general, therefore, the leader needs to understand where they are starting from and what needs to be done *immediately* in order to start moving in the right direction. It is worth remembering that everyone can develop their leadership potential, and authority: trust and respect are there to be earned.

Understand your own leadership style and recognise the different leadership needs of individuals

It is vitally important for successful leadership to match the leadership style to both the situation and the people involved. For example:

- *Close involvement, with a high level of directing and monitoring by the leader –* this is often most effective with people who are unable or unwilling to take responsibility (although in the longer term the solution for the leader is to address the root causes of *why* the individual works this

way, and work towards changing their pattern of behaviour or position so that they are comfortable and willing to take responsibility).
- *A coaching approach* – this works best with people who lack confidence, but show signs of potential. The goal is gradually to get them to take on more responsibility and start realising their potential, and this is best achieved by coaching, directing and supporting their actions, and reinforcing their successes.
- *Communicating clearly and regularly* is usually the best approach when dealing with talented under-achievers: this is designed to get them on the right track and unblock whatever obstacles have prevented success. Their views need to be sought and they should share in the decision-making and be encouraged to take the initiative.

Finally, successful, fully competent high achievers should be left alone – if it ain't broke don't fix it! However, it is worth monitoring their work, remaining ready to offer support and ensuring that they are heading in the right direction.

Lead from the front, by example

It is important to confirm yourself as leader, building trust and respect, by setting a clear example to your team. This means treating others as you would wish to be treated and developing a range of attributes such as: demonstrating good work habits; understanding and valuing your staff's work; handling pressure; clearly demonstrating the values and aims that you hold dear; encouraging initiative and enthusiasm; providing regular, considered feedback, and listening and learning.

> **Summary:** *Leadership skills*
>
> Decisiveness, vision, understanding and confidence are at the core of successful leadership. The leader needs to be able to use these qualities combined with additional skills relevant to each situation. The best leaders communicate their vision clearly and often: they are open to new approaches and ideas, but they know the direction in which the team and organisation should be heading. They create a vision, communicate it and guide their team to achieve it.

Further information

Strategy and Leadership
B. Leavy and D. Wilson, Wiley and Sons, 1994

Successful Leadership in a Week
Carol O'Connor, Hodder Headline, 1994

Improving Leadership Performance
P. Wright and D. Taylor, Prentice Hall, 1994

On Becoming a Leader
W. Bennis, Hutchinson Business, 1989

Leadership Skills
J. Adair, Institute of Personnel and Development, 1997

Leadership styles and organisational culture

Introduction

The style in which a leader approaches their task can be critical to success. Behaviours and attitudes that are effective in one organisation or situation may be wholly inappropriate in another. Leadership style is determined by a number of factors:

- *Norms of society* – the types of behaviour that one is familiar with influences one's leadership style. So, for example, many western managers find it extremely difficult to apply their usual management practices and leadership style in China, because of the wholly different style and approach of the Chinese.
- *Nature and purpose of the organisation* – leadership style is affected by what the organisation does, so a style appropriate for a top security prison would probably not work so well in a kindergarten (or maybe it would …).
- *The specific type of situation* – for example, the style adopted by a leader during a crisis will be different from that adopted during an interview – or it should be!

Closely linked is the issue of *organisational culture* which enjoys a symbiotic relationship with leadership style, each influencing the other and determining what is done, how it is done and what level of success results. This section examines the relevance of differing styles of leadership for varying situations, and how the issue of style and approach underpins effective leadership. It also provides an overview of types of organisational culture.

Situational leadership

Paul Hersey and Ken Blanchard developed the *situational leadership model*, which shattered the belief that there is one ideal leadership style suitable for all situations. Their view, which built on the Blake Mouton Managerial Grid, is shown in Figure 1 and is that leaders need to adapt their leadership style to the needs of each specific situation.

Situational leadership matrix

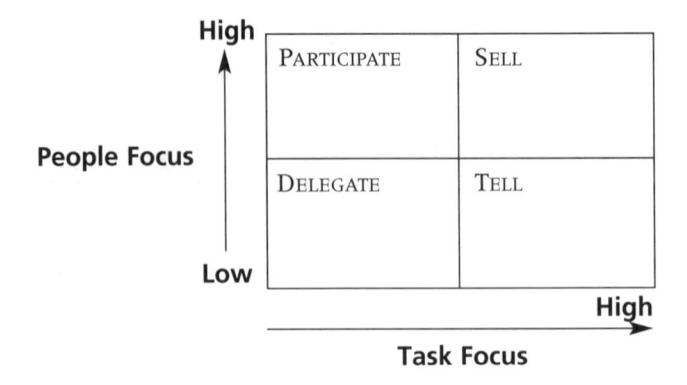

	Low Task Focus	High Task Focus
High People Focus	Participate	Sell
Low People Focus	Delegate	Tell

Figure 1 Situational leadership

For Hersey and Blanchard, leadership style rests on two factors:

1. *The emphasis that the leader places on the task (task focus).* In general, the more task-focused a leader is the more *directive* and action-oriented their behaviour will be. Hersey and Blanchard also focused on *output variables* on this axis, meaning measurable short- to medium-term performance indicators such as net profits, revenues, production figures, etc..
2. *The emphasis that the leader places on the relationship with the people (people focus).* Leaders who emphasise their relationship with their staff tend to be more *supportive*, empowering and enabling. They also emphasised the importance of *intervening variables* on this axis, by which they meant the intangible aspects of long-term success such as communications, decision-making, creativity, etc..

This matrix results in four different leadership styles:

1. Telling (or authoritative)
2. Selling (or involved)
3. Participating (or caring)
4. Uninvolved (or delegate).

These styles are used by the leader at different times, as appropriate, and the leader can switch between styles to suit the needs of the task and the people involved (for further information about the stages of team development see TEAM-BUILDING AND LEADING HIGH-PERFORMING TEAMS).

LEADERSHIP STYLES AND ORGANISATIONAL CULTURE

Leadership style	Characteristics
Participating • Low task, high relationship	• Suitable for a situation in which a mature team continues to function well (the norming and performing stage of team development – see TEAM-BUILDING AND LEADING HIGH-PERFORMING TEAMS). • The leader has delegated and empowered their staff and is no longer involved in short-term performance and operational measures (to do so would offend the team's expertise and sense of commitment). • The longer-term matters, and the leader focuses on individual and team development, planning and innovation.
Selling • High task, high relationship	• Suitable when the team has worked together for some time and has developed understanding and expertise (the norming stage of team development). • Works when a balance is needed between short- and long-term aspects. The leader needs to monitor the achievement of targets, but longer-term elements such as communication networks and decision-making processes are also important.
Delegating • Low task, low relationship	• A 'hands-off' style that works best with a highly experienced, successful team (the performing stage of team development). • The team works well with very little involvement from the leader; instead the leadership role is often to work externally for the team, developing networks, gaining resources, spreading best practice and expertise from the team across the organisation as a whole. • Leaders may intervene in the team if requested to help define problems and devise solutions, or if a problem arises (in which case the leader may switch to the participating style).

Leadership style	Characteristics
Telling • High task, low relationship	• This situation works when the team is new, temporary or forming (the forming and storming stages of team development). • The leader is hands-on, decisive and involved with the needs of the task and the team. They direct the team and stress the importance of tasks and deadlines. This can then ultimately move on to the selling style as the team grows in confidence and competence.

Table 5 Leadership styles

Autocracy, democracy and delegation

The three most frequently cited leadership stereotypes are listed below. Normally during training courses, individuals will balk at one or two of these as being entirely unreasonable, even unprofessional, because they do not sit with the individual's preferred way of working. In fact, many successful leaders use all three styles: the key to success being seen as knowing *when* each style is appropriate.

Autocracy

Characteristics of autocratic leadership include:

- making all decisions, prescribing solutions and giving detailed instructions;
- exerting close control and suppressing conflict;
- one-way communications.

The one great advantage of autocracy is that decisions are made quickly, which can be vital in extreme situations, e.g. soldiers in battle or the emergency services dealing with a crisis. If the leader is able to decide correctly, and the team is willing to follow their leader, then autocracy is also the most cost-effective style. Democracy, by contrast, carries an overhead: it takes time to involve people. Autocracy can work well occasionally, for certain short-term tasks and in specific situations: not all tasks involve long-term goals, and not all teams need developing.

Democracy

Characteristics of a democratic leader include:

LEADERSHIP STYLES AND ORGANISATIONAL CULTURE

- Listening, supporting, encouraging, trusting and developing the team.
- Involving, co-ordinating and committing people.
- Providing direction whilst at the same time including others in key decisions.
- Motivating the team through long-term tasks, keeping control of the team and guiding, directing and supporting.
- The humility or self-confidence to understand their own limitations and seek the advice of others.

Determination and concern for others usually characterise this style of leadership, and it has gained in popularity over recent years as the importance of empowerment and mentoring in particular has risen, and as organisations have become much less hierarchical (with flatter structures) and more technically specialised. Democracy works over the long term where people's development matters most (both for their motivation and the organisation's success); it is also vital for innovative projects or new developments where the leader's experience is no greater (and possibly less) than their team's.

Delegating leadership

Characteristics of a delegating leader include:

- Giving little direction
- Being uncritical and avoiding conflict
- Trusting.

Leading from the front, by example, sometimes involves trusting the leadership of the team to someone else who is more competent to manage a particular situation. This can be a high-risk strategy, but often the greater risk is for the leader to assume that their position is immovable and to make mistakes that they can actually *see* coming. Delegating leadership requires confidence and trust within the team, and usually occurs in well-established teams facing new or complex situations (an example would be NASA missions into space). *Comfort zones* – in many jobs the ideal style can shift from autocratic to democratic or delegative, and then back again. Leaders who can perform well in all of these functions are often the most valuable to an organisation and are quite rare. The keys to the leader extending their comfort zone and applying the best leadership style lie in *flexibility* and *practice*: the more the leader uses each style the better prepared they are.

Styles of problem analysis and decision-making (Myers Briggs type inventory)

The Myers Briggs type inventory is a popular tool for identifying personality types, and is particularly powerful for assessing different styles of problem analysis and decision-making. Established over fifty years ago, the inventory is based on the works of the Swiss psychoanalyst Carl Jung. Jung's view was that there are four dimensions to people's behaviour, and each dimension has two opposing characteristics, as follows:

1. Extraversion (E) ——————— vs ——————— Introversion (I)
2. Sensing (S) ——————— vs ——————— Intuition (N)
3. Thinking (T) ——————— vs ——————— Feeling (F)
4. Judging (J) ——————— vs ——————— Perceiving (P)

Of course people will have elements of both opposing behaviours, but the point is that they will naturally *prefer* working in one mode rather than the other. The value of the Myers Briggs inventory is that it highlights the way that people act, helping individuals to understand their leadership, problem-solving and decision-making style. In understanding their preferred mode of working leaders can see where they need to develop and gaps that they may need to fill. For example, an introvert boss may welcome an extrovert deputy that brings a different style and approach to the team.

The inventory itself assesses individuals against each of the four dimensions, highlighting the styles that people tend to prefer:

1. How we derive energy

- *Extraversion* – an outward perspective that provides scope and dynamism; or
- *Introversion* – a more introspective and reflecting approach that emphasises intellect in problem-solving.

2. How we obtain information

- *Sensing* – an approach that emphasises empirical evidence, facts and experience; organised; or
- *Intuition* – an emphasis on the opportunities in a situation, inventive, focused on future possibilities rather than past precedent, less structured.

3. How we make decisions

- *Thinking* – logical, structured, dispassionate, objective, skilled at analysis and understanding facts; or
- *Feeling* – closely involved, empathetic, subjective, excels at understanding people.

4. How we organise and structure what we do

- *Judging* – planning, structuring and organising so that problems can be tackled in an orderly, prepared and decisive manner; or

- *Perceiving* – generating and exploring ideas, being autonomous, keeping flexible and relaxed.

As well as helping individuals to understand their own preferred styles for problem-solving, the Myers Briggs inventory is also invaluable in a range of other situations, including team-building, where there is a need to assess the working styles of other people and ensure that a balance exists.

Organisational culture

It has been stressed that no single aspect of an organisation can be viewed in isolation: each feature interacts to provide a given level of performance. One of the key features affecting leadership style and performance is *culture* – the complex mix of personal and social attitudes, values and relationships.

There are various ways to characterise an organisation's culture; one of the most popular and commonly used was developed by Charles Handy, and classifies culture types by the dominant concern within the organisation. These culture-types are:

- Club culture
- Role culture
- Task culture
- Person culture.

The four types can mix within organisations – for example, some departments or teams may work and be led entirely differently from others – but the prevailing culture will influence leadership style, and vice versa.

Club culture

This is often shown as a spider's web where the leader is the central source of power, surrounded by ever-widening circles of influence.

- Lines of communication are short: little is formally written down and instead personal contact is often the way that ideas are conveyed.
- The major *strength* of this culture is the speed with which the organisation can respond intuitively to opportunities and generally to change. The **weakness** is the dominance of the single, central figure.
- A central factor in the success of this culture is a core of like-minded people – hence the club analogy.

Role culture

This style of organisation is managed with an emphasis on set procedures, rules, hierarchy and formal communications. People work according to carefully defined, rigid job descriptions, which detail the requirements of the role and its boundaries.

- Role cultures tend to feature prominently in mature organisations as well as large organisations.
- The *strength* of role cultures is their effectiveness in completing routine or repetitive tasks. The *weakness* is their inflexibility and inability to cope with change. They can also stifle creativity and innovation.

Task culture

Task cultures involve teams whose skills are applied to a specific problem, project or task. Organisations are often structured in a matrix with groups forming and reforming to complete tasks and achieve objectives.

- The focus is firmly on completing the task successfully.
- The main sources of power fluctuate, depending on the expertise required and available for each specific task – and the level of success achieved.
- The *strength* is the problem-solving, forward-looking, 'can do' way that the organisation channels skills and expertise into completing the task. This flexibility results in an ability to cope well with challenges and change. The *weakness* of this structure can be its unsuitability to consistently repeat tasks and processes.

Person culture

The last of Handy's four culture types differs from the others in that instead of people being grouped to meet the objectives of the organisation, the organisation exists to meet the needs of the individual. This type of culture is highly individualistic and is most often seen among professionals, such as barristers' chambers or doctors grouped for convenience into practices. In this environment there is a lack of identifiable power as the structure is so highly individualistic, and the strengths and weaknesses are clearly those of the individual.

> **Case study:** *Individual leadership style*
>
> A Finance Director that I once worked with had a very unusual leadership style. He worked for a lively, innovative and successful management consultancy with bright, enthusiastic young people all implementing the very latest management techniques. Yet he was quiet to the point of being reserved, and never ventured a view on management

techniques or philosophies. Instead, he came to work at 7 am, left at 7 pm and stayed in his office virtually the whole time (except when he went to meetings, which he hated!).

Despite his odd appearance (he chain-smoked and looked rather unconventional) he was very highly regarded by everyone in the firm – something I could not understand when I first met him. However, the reason for his strong reputation soon became evident: he was always calm, perceptive and positive – indeed, that was where most of his energies went. If he disagreed or disapproved he would simply shake his head; if he disagreed vehemently he would shake his head and say no; and if he was implacably opposed to something he would shake his head, say no and fix you with a determined smile. It never failed, and it never failed to impress those who worked with him. It certainly helped that he was capable and knew what he was doing, but even when mistakes were made – his or yours – he was the same: positive, encouraging and with ample common sense. He completely lacked charisma, but his focus on the needs of tasks, teams and individuals ensured that his views were always sought, even on topics far outside his own specific area of finance.

Summary: *Leadership style and culture*

Leadership style and culture are closely interrelated, each affecting the other, but what also links them is the importance to the organisation of the *mix* of each factor. Getting the right leadership style for a specific task or circumstance is essential – the approach of situational leadership – and the leader can move between styles as needed to ensure success. Similarly, getting the right blend of culture in an organisation increases its effectiveness and chances of succeeding, and the right blend depends on the issues and level of change facing the organisation, as well as the intrinsic level of skills and attitude that the staff possess. No style is *the* best, and no culture is *the* best, only the best at a given time.

Further information

Gods of Management
C. Handy, Pan, 1995

A Force for Change: How leadership differs from management
J. Kotter, Free Press, 1990

Improving Leadership Effectiveness: The leader match concept
F. Fiedler and M. Chemers, John Wiley and Sons, 1994

Leading for the first time

> **Introduction**
>
> Every day thousands – if not millions – of people start out as a leader for the first time. It is universally nerve-wracking and people are invariably unprepared. However, the key to avoiding worry is exactly the same as the key to achieving success: plan, prepare and focus on what you need to do to be successful. This advice is applicable for people starting any new job – not necessarily leading for the first time.

Succeeding as a new leader

Focusing on your own situation

Success requires a range of measures and different approaches, and in all of these it is important to feel comfortable with your approach and develop your own style. Understanding your own weaknesses and ways of working is therefore an essential first step in developing the skills needed. It can be helpful for new leaders to consider their strengths in the following broad areas:

- *Managing yourself* – managing time and stress, influencing people, handling and resolving conflict, setting and achieving personal targets, communicating effectively, understanding your leadership style.
- *Managing people* – empowering, delegating, mentoring, coaching, team-building, recruiting, supporting, disciplining, creating conditions for people to be motivated and succeed, establishing and reinforcing the values of the organisation, influencing the organisational culture.
- *Managing operations, information and resources* – analysing, problem-solving, decision-making, negotiating, planning, handling technology.
- *Setting a clear vision, direction and then gaining people's commitment,* mobilising them to achieve the desired goals.
- *Managing and controlling finance* – understanding financial tools and techniques, setting financial objectives and controlling financial performance.
- *Initiating change* so that the organisation is in a state of continuous improvement.

Once you have decided where you need to improve your skills, the next stage is to plan *how* and *when* this development will occur. A personal development plan can be a valuable asset in achieving this. As well as reviewing areas for development it is also useful to reflect on your leadership style (and how you have worked in the past). For example, an introverted boss often finds an extraverted deputy a considerable asset; or an analytical leader benefits from the support of more active, practical individuals. The important point is to understand how you work best and then create the necessary environment in which you can succeed.

Often it is useful to seek support, calling on an informal mentor or peer who can provide information, help and even guidance if the leader is new to the organisation. This support mechanism can be invaluable for removing many of the minor worries that can be distracting. The leader's boss may be suitable, but often a different perspective can be helpful.

The new leader needs to understand that their mode of working, and probably everything about them, will be closely watched. It is therefore important to start as you mean to go on and be consistent. Team members may be wary, concerned, keen to impress, or have any number of other approaches and issues for the new leader. The key point is to adopt the style and values from the start that you want to continue with. If necessary and appropriate, explain what these are, how you work and what you intend to achieve.

Closely linked with the need to set the right tone from the start is the need to hit current *and potential* problems hard and early. A sign of good leadership is a willingness to lead from the front, by example, tackling and resolving problems. The advantages of this are:

- it shows determination and sends a clear message;
- it displays the leader's style and approach, as well as their skills and ability;
- it can often generate respect, trust and authority;
- it removes the problem and makes life easier.

Setting clear objectives for what you want to achieve personally is also important in sustaining performance and achieving success. As a leader it is useful to develop a set of objectives or goals for the short, medium and long term. As well as developing these goals it is useful to reflect on how they will be achieved, and then regularly review how they are progressing. Once accomplished new goals should be added. This process has a number of advantages:

- It helps to provide a long-term perspective at a time when the new leader can be preoccupied with the present, providing a touchstone for the leader.

- It motivates and provides a focus for action.
- It challenges and sustains the leader.

Focusing on the team

As well as setting your personal objectives, it is also important for the new leader to swiftly establish clear objectives for the team. The role of the leader is to *lead,* and this means focusing on the needs of the task, team and individuals. Clear objectives for each individual will ensure that the team understands what is required and will move in the right (and the same!) direction to accomplish the task.

A valuable way of gaining commitment, establishing authority and achieving success as a new leader is to *create early successes.* Starting as a leader can be unsettling and demanding for everyone. Early successes provide motivation, create a team spirit, set an example and lead to new opportunities.

It is also necessary for the leader to understand the team's needs and to provide support. The new leader needs to understand which stage of development the team has reached: forming, storming, norming, performing or reforming (see TEAM-BUILDING AND LEADING HIGH-PERFORMING TEAMS). The needs of a newly formed team will be quite different from a more experienced one. It is also worth getting one – or more – external perspectives on the team, helping to understand their strengths and weaknesses. Providing support may mean:

- representing the team externally and arguing their case;
- reviewing resource requirements;
- helping individuals to develop to their full potential.

Keeping the overall picture in view, as well as the detail

It is often easy for the new leader to fall into the trap of being dragged into the detail of completing tasks or reacting to events, rather than leading and setting direction. It is therefore important to review the situation and progress during the early days; checking how things are going, perhaps with an appraisal with the leader's boss or through discussions with individual team members (usually after the first month and before the third). Another approach is to get the views of an outsider – although these may be too distant to provide a detailed assessment. This should help guide and focus the new leader, building confidence, showing areas for attention and checking that all is on track.

It helps as a new leader to master the details. This includes detailed aspects of the job, as that shows the team and others that details matter; it very often engenders trust and understanding among individuals when the leader remembers details.

The final aspect of successfully developing as a new leader is to reconcile home and work demands. Leading for the first time can be highly demanding – and leadership itself is an isolating activity – therefore, support from friends and family is invaluable. However, it is also important to remember that home life too needs to be supported, it is a two-way relationship, and the new leader needs to make time to ensure that work and home life are in balance. Friends and family can often provide a useful external perspective, as well as an opportunity to relax and refresh your approach. The danger is either to assume that home life will look after itself or that relationships can take any amount of neglect: often they cannot, and problems from home will affect performance at work.

Summary: *Checklist for the new leader*

1. Consider your own situation.
2. Devise a plan for your own personal development.
3. Understand your own personal style of leadership.
4. Seek support.
5. Start as you mean to go on.
6. Hit current *and* potential problems hard and early.
7. Set clear objectives for what you want to achieve personally.
8. Set clear objectives for the team.
9. Create early successes.
10. Understand the team's needs and provide support.
11. Review the situation and your progress during the early days.
12. Pay attention to detail.
13. Reconcile home and work demands.

Further information

On Becoming a Leader
W. Bennis, Hutchinson Business, 1989

Leading Change
John Kotter, Harvard Business School Press, 1996

The Successful Boss's First 100 Days
R. Koch, FT/Pitman, 1994

80 Things You Must do to be a Great Boss
D. Fremantle, McGraw-Hill, 1993

Successful Leadership in a Week
Carol O'Connor, Hodder Headline, 1994

Leading other leaders

Introduction

Leading other leaders can be daunting and it often needs a different style from leading a team of less experienced or more junior personnel, but the essential characteristics of leadership should remain the same. These include:

- building trust and respect;
- challenging and stimulating the leader;
- empowering the leader and giving them as much latitude as possible;
- communicating your message clearly;
- demonstrating support;
- mentoring and counselling.

However, as well as differences in style there also needs to be a difference in emphasis. For example, it is clearly very important to remember that the subordinate has leadership responsibilities overlaid on their roles and to take care not to undermine them. Indeed, the opposite is true: the person in charge should proactively look for ways to reinforce the subordinate's position as a leader.

Leading leaders requires a difference in emphasis in other ways, depending on the needs of the task and team. For example, it is quite normal for leaders to act in a mentoring capacity with subordinates who are also leaders. This recognises that leadership at any level can be a lonely activity, and rather than help them to do their job in general the 'overall boss' should help them to be a more effective leader. This may include providing an alternative perspective on specific problems or issues; reflecting key questions to help the subordinate think through issues, or simply providing the benefit of their experience as a leader.

Finally, perhaps more than any other aspect of leadership, a strong personal rapport is often valuable for success. The converse is also true: a poor personal rapport will often cause problems for both sides – and the organisation as a whole. This relationship does not necessarily need to be friendship (although that helps), but there does need to be a strong element of mutual respect.

Key points for effectively leading leaders

The techniques needed for leading people who are themselves leaders are very largely the same as for leading anyone else, with several notable additions.

Other leaders should be granted as much freedom to lead and manage as possible

This includes, where feasible, the opportunity to decide *what* is to be implemented as well as *how*. Other leaders must have the freedom to decide how best to achieve what you (or the organisation) requires of them. However, it is often not possible to separate *what* needs to be achieved from *how* it will be achieved. The overall leader therefore needs to involve others in deciding what is to be achieved. Although ultimate responsibility will still rest with the overall leader, this approach has the advantage of gaining commitment (avoiding the not-invented-here syndrome) and understanding.

Show trust and support

It is important to remember that the best results are achieved when people are trusted with their responsibilities and shown support. This may be easy to say and agree, but can require superhuman levels of faith, patience and understanding in practice! The extent to which trust and support must be exercised by leaders is possibly the most controversial aspect of the whole topic. My personal view, based on my own experiences and also observing, studying and interviewing other leaders, is as follows:

- Trust and support must always be given by one leader to another in public, on the grounds that massive harm will be done to the subordinate's individual confidence and their long-term ability to lead if it is not.
- When disagreeing with someone in private consider two interrelated questions: first, how will this person respond to being overruled? Second, is the long-term harm that will be caused by this disagreement greater or smaller than the long-term benefit that will result from having my own way?
- If you disagree with another leader they must be given the opportunity and support to explain this and then move on, ideally securing some quick, high-profile successes that will reinforce their value and worth both to themselves and everyone else.

However, there are extreme situations when this will not work. A surgeon or soldier, for example, may need to disagree on the spot with a subordinate in front of others. These situations should be the exception, and when they do occur people tend to understand that they are extremes and are an integral part of the job, thus reducing or removing any long-term consequences.

Support leaders and empower them to create change

When you are empowering other leaders to create major change the following points are especially relevant:

- *Communicate a sensible vision to employees* – if employees have a shared sense of purpose, it will be easier to initiate actions to achieve that purpose.
- *Make structures compatible with the vision* – ensure that the system allows change to be effected, and that any obstacles to change are removed. It is also necessary to align information and personnel systems so that they are compatible with the planned outcome.
- *Provide the training that people need* – without the right skills and attitudes, people feel disempowered.
- *Confront people who undercut needed change* – nothing disempowers people the way a bad boss can: the solution is to confront them and take action, rather than let the situation continue breeding ill-feeling and problems.

Consider how best to challenge and develop leaders

A common mistake is to assume that as leaders have already achieved a measure of success (if only by becoming a leader), they do not need challenging opportunities or professional development. Life-long learning is an essential aspect of successful leadership, and leaders should be encouraged to develop their skills just like anyone else. Some areas where leaders might benefit can include:

- *Risk-taking* – developing a willingness to push out of comfort zones. The rules for risk-taking need to be clear, and there will need to be a blame-free environment, but encouraging leaders to take risks can unlock a great deal of experience, intuition and success.
- *Humble self-reflection* – honestly assessing successes and failures, especially the latter, is not always easy for leaders, who may be given to moving on quickly, preferring to bury or leave behind their mistakes. However, analysing them can provide important clues about what to do in the future, as well as highlighting the leader's own strengths and weaknesses.
- *Solicitation of opinions* – 360 degree appraisal is a process whereby the views of one's subordinates, peers and bosses are collected and acted upon. This too can highlight areas to be improved or reinforced.

- *Careful listening and openness to new ideas* – occasionally leaders are not good listeners, preferring instead to lead from the front or to shoulder all of the responsibility themselves. This may *appear* necessary, particularly if others are inexperienced, but by genuinely canvassing opinions and listening to others new ideas and perspectives will often emerge. Perhaps the leader needs to be encouraged to listen to their colleagues more.

> **Summary:** *Allow leaders a greater degree of latitude*
>
> Leadership can often be a lonely activity – and shutting people out can make it even lonelier both for you and them. Again, the extent to which you grant freedom and latitude depends on your leadership style, but letting people do some or all of the following will probably help to bring out their best. Consider letting people:
>
> - Follow up their own initiatives and interesting new ideas, without necessarily consulting you (or setting parameters where they do not have to consult).
> - Decide how they will pursue their own professional development.
> - Manage their own resources, particularly staff and money.
> - Make mistakes in a blame-free environment.
> - Challenge you on anything you do that affects their work.
> - Manage their own work environment.
> - Develop their own individual leadership style. This will involve them developing their own style of team leadership, handling poor performers etc..
> - Take the lead in monitoring and reviewing their own performance.
> - Know that you support them.

Further information

Leadership
J.M. Burns, Harper and Row, 1978

Leading Change
John Kotter, Harvard Business School Press, 1996

Frontiers of Leadership: An essential reader
M. Syrett and C. Hogg (Editors), Blackwell, 1992

Managing finance and profitability

> **Introduction**
>
> Financial management is an area that many business leaders fear more than any other: it is frequently neglected and left to the accounting experts. Yet every commercial enterprise has two vital requirements – to generate a profit, and to generate sufficient cash (the life-blood of any business) to continue trading. Without *profit* the investors that can sustain the business will withdraw and there will be nothing to reinvest in the business. Without *cash* death comes even quicker: the business is unable to settle its accounts and becomes insolvent. Financial management and profitability are therefore vital for survival and success, and financial leadership is an essential aspect of business leadership in general.
>
> It should be emphasised that there are many excellent, detailed books available that demystify financial management techniques. This section highlights some of the most useful and popular terms and techniques, helping to equip the profit-driven manager with the necessary skills for successful financial leadership.

Understanding key financial terms and statements

Financial leadership requires an understanding of key terms and definitions, and some of the most significant are explained below.

Key terms used in financial statements

Within balance sheets and financial statements in general, there are a number of terms that frequently appear and must be clearly understood:

- *Fixed assets* – these are assets (or resources), such as buildings, land, plant, equipment, fixtures and fittings, that are stated at cost less accumulated depreciation. In the case of buildings or land the figure stated may result from a professional valuation. Most assets are *tangible assets* (e.g. equipment, buildings, etc..), but increasingly businesses are also valuing *intangible assets* such as goodwill and brands.
- *Current assets* – these can often be thought of as more transitory assets such as raw materials, work in progress and finished goods; debtors

(people that owe money to the business); deposits and short-term investments, and cash.
- *Creditors* – creditors divide into two categories: *creditors due within one year*, which usually consist of short-term borrowings such as overdrafts; current instalments of loans, and other amounts owed by the company, for example to suppliers. The second category is *creditors due after more than one year*, consisting mainly of secured and unsecured loans, and obligations under finance leases for the purchase of fixed assets.
- *Net current assets* – are current assets less creditors due within one year.
- *Called up share capital* – consists of ordinary, and in certain instances, preference share, both listed at nominal value. (Share options are excluded until the shares are allotted to directors and staff.)
- *Retained profit* – this is all of the profit retained in the company after the payment of tax and share dividends, since the formation of the company. It is used to provide additional finance for the business.
- *Reserves* – include retained profits (where appropriate they may also include share premium account and property revaluation).
- *Stocks* – these include: raw materials and consumables; work-in-progress, and finished goods for resale. Stocks are always valued prudently at whichever figure is lower: their cost, or the amount they can be sold for (their net realisable value).
- *Debtors* – are normally *trade debtors* or customers that owe the business money.
- *Depreciation* – this is charged on tangible fixed assets, excluding land, as well as intangible assets owned by a company. The purpose of depreciation is to allow for the decline in value of an asset. The most commonly used method for calculating depreciation is to write off the cost of the asset evenly over its estimated useful life, where appropriate taking into account any residual value that will be realised when the asset is sold (or disposed). Significantly for cash management, depreciation does not mean setting cash aside to replace the asset in due course, it is simply a means of calculating the asset's value at a given point in time.

Balance sheet

The balance sheet is published in the company's Annual Report and provides a 'snapshot' picture of the company's financial performance at the end of the year. In particular, the balance sheet shows:

- how much capital is employed in the business;
- how quickly the assets can be turned into cash (the liquidity of the business);
- how solvent the business is; and

- how the business is financed.

Balance sheets are increasingly used by management accountants for internal use, showing the company's position at a particular point in time (e.g. month end, quarter end, or before a major transaction such as a merger or acquisition). In essence, the balance sheet shows the value of the company by highlighting its assets and liabilities. With comparative figures for the previous period it can also show trends in the company's fortunes, and this is important when monitoring how well and aggressively assets and profits are being managed.

It should be remembered that because balance sheets show a number of important factors (such as the value of assets, creditors in total and for a specific period, called-up share capital, reserves) there are slightly different formats that are used, depending on what (and who) the balance sheet is for.

Profit and loss account

The profit and loss account has to be published annually by the company, but it is frequently used as a tool to manage the finances of the business. The profit and loss account highlights:

- the turnover or sales for the period
- expenditure for the period
- the profit (or loss, which is shown in parentheses)
- how the profit was divided.

The profit or loss is calculated by taking the *revenue* that has been invoiced but not necessarily paid during the period (also known as sales turnover or fee income), and deducting the *costs* incurred to produce that sales turnover (but not necessarily paid during the period), and the *depreciation* charged on assets owned within the business. An important point to note is that profit and cash are very different. The cash is what is at hand in the bank, whereas the profit is the sum of what has been received and paid out during the year, plus depreciation.

As with the balance sheet, there are variations on the format that can be used for a profit and loss account. Also, again as with the balance sheet, the profit and loss account (or P&L) should be read in conjunction with the notes to the accounts, as these explain the accounting policies used and shed light on some of the background to how the figures were calculated.

The P&L account shows how well the business is trading, and can highlight important areas of success (e.g. high sales) and weakness (e.g. high costs, or low revenue despite high sales, which may indicate a pricing or discounting problem). The P&L is particularly useful if you are worried about high overhead charges and costs, as it gives a breakdown of each expense.

In essence, the P&L shows *whether* corrective action is needed to maximise profit, and can also suggest *where* that action might be best targeted (e.g. pricing; which cost elements need to be controlled, or sales volumes).

Source and application of funds statement

UK companies are required to publish a *source and application of funds statement* annually (in addition to a balance sheet and profit and loss account). The statement shows:

- the source of funds generated (e.g. share issues, profit before tax);
- the use of funds applied (e.g. purchase of fixed assets, increased stocks and debtors, tax and dividends paid).

Cash flow forecast

The most important of all financial statements, particularly for small and medium-sized businesses but also highly relevant to large companies, is the cash flow forecast. Many businesses make the fatal mistake of focusing on profit, ignoring the fact that cash is the life-blood of the business. Knowing how much cash will be needed is particularly important for new businesses and provides an essential aspect of the overall business plan, not only for keeping on track but for gaining and maintaining the support of financial backers (e.g. shareholders and banks).

Forecasting the cash needs of a business is therefore essential, and there are a number of vital points that should be remembered when preparing and using a cash flow:

- *Structure* – the cash flow forecast needs to be structured in a table, with receipts and payments set against the month that they occur, showing the flow of money in and out of the business. The forecast is divided into three separate sections:

    1. *Receipts* or money coming into the business. This includes cash, debtors, value added tax and loans.
    2. *Payments* including trade creditors, wages, overheads, equipment, loan repayments, overdraft interest, drawings or staff costs, tax.
    3. *Balances* – these are the monthly as well as the cumulative balances.

(Note that non-cash items such as depreciation are excluded: they may affect profitability but they do not, at least in the short-term, affect the ability of the business to trade.)

- *Preparation* – when you prepare the forecast you will probably need to prepare a budget for the business for the year ahead. The first step is to fill in your predictable payments (e.g. staff, advertising). The next step

MANAGING FINANCE AND PROFITABILITY

is to estimate likely sales revenues, and include the time that the cash will be *received*, not when it will be invoiced. From the sales forecast you can then calculate and include costs of sale, the direct costs (such as raw materials) that are related to levels of sales and production. Finally, remember to include figures for the month in which they will *actually* be received or paid.

- *Using the cash flow forecast* – the cash flow is valuable for determining *how much* cash the business needs; *when* you might need additional cash, for example in the form of loans; and *what you can afford to spend* (for example on staff costs). It is particularly important to be cautious when anticipating cash flows, especially when starting a business.

Case study: *The dangers of increasing turnover*

A production manager worked for a manufacturing company producing circuit boards for domestic appliances. His job was suddenly made much harder when the sales department extended customers' payment terms in order to get more business. The result was a sudden surge of orders – and little cash or credit to pay suppliers to meet them. The production manager then had to prepare a cash flow forecast with the finance department (to allow money to be borrowed from the bank); prioritise supplies and suppliers, and renegotiate the company's payment terms with suppliers.

Some of the suppliers agreed to the extended payment terms, in effect letting the circuit board manufacturer get paid before paying their suppliers, but in return they demanded either a guarantee of work at a fixed price for 12 months, or higher prices for the goods they supplied. In addition, interest rates were high and this was reflected in the overdraft from the bank. That year's financial accounts for the circuit board manufacturer saw a 25 per cent increase in turnover and only a 3 per cent increase in profits, due to rising costs.

A better approach might have been to plan the sales offer of extended payment terms: check first with suppliers that it was feasible; ensure that there would be sufficient cash on hand to pay for supplies, and consider offsetting the extended payment terms with an increase in sales prices.

Techniques for effective financial control

Budgeting and budgetary control

Budgets are a common part of business management, but frequently they are not used to their full potential (and in many cases are completely resented!). A budget is best seen as a tactical plan to achieve worthwhile objectives (such as for revenue, profit or shareholder value). The key elements for successful budgeting are that the budget meets the strategic and operational objectives, and most importantly of all these include sales (or revenue) targets. Another vital element in using budgets for financial control is that you can monitor actual results against budget, and you have the necessary systems in place to allow you to monitor financial performance routinely. The time should be taken in analysis, deciding what corrective action to take and taking it – getting the figures right in the first instance should be the easiest part of the process!

- *The sales budget* – this is the foundation for the budget and the business, and is essential for getting the right organisation of resources. It should include the number of units to be sold at a given price, including discount, and may be broken down by timing, area, product line, etc. It needs to be a realistic assessment of likely sales, based on the best available market research. Sales budgets are ideally produced on a monthly or quarterly basis, as well as in an annual format, so that progress and expectations can be checked and updated regularly.
- *The total production budget* – the production budget follows the sales budget, and includes direct costs or those that depend directly on the level of sales. Other costs may also be included such as sales commission, to give an estimate for cost of sales. The production budget is useful to know for managing suppliers and ensuring that you have the right resources ready at the right time.
- *The overhead budget* – overheads vary considerably: they can be relatively low in manufacturing industries or high for service businesses, and include fixed costs such as staff costs, telephone, premises. Depending on the type of business, they can be allocated for each product or alternatively budgeted as an overall figure for the business. The important point is to choose the most useful approach and be consistent.

When budgeting it is worth remembering that:

1. It is best to budget early so that you know your likely financial requirements.

MANAGING FINANCE AND PROFITABILITY

2. You need to consider carefully the best period to budget for (normally a year).
3. Your budgets may be of interest to others outside the normal running of the business (such as bankers).
4. Budgets provide a valuable starting point for preparing the cash flow forecast.

Costing and profit management

Financial leadership requires entrepreneurial, profit-driven management, and this in turn means understanding and applying standard costing terms and techniques, such as fixed and variable costs, and break-even analysis.

- *Variable costs* – are costs that increase or decrease in direct proportion to changes in sales volume. Examples of variable costs include the materials used to make a product, or royalties payable on each sale. Generally, variable costs are most susceptible to control by people at all levels of the business, and their relationship to revenue should be closely monitored (this is achieved by monitoring the gross profit margin – see **Using financial ratios to manage profitability**, below).
- *Fixed costs* – remain unchanged in the short term despite changes in sales volume. These costs tend to be related to *time* rather than volume, and include monthly staff costs or monthly expenses such as rent, lighting, heating. Controlling these costs tends to be the responsibility of more senior managers within an organisation, and they should be managed carefully: reducing them is usually more difficult and has significant implications for the whole of the business (e.g. reducing staffing levels or moving premises). However, if that is where the problems lie and the business is carrying a level of fixed overhead that is too great, then that is where action needs to be taken.
- *Break-even analysis* – the break-even point is the level of sales at which neither a profit nor a loss results. It can be calculated as follows:

$$\text{Break-even point} = \frac{\text{costs}}{\text{gross profit per cent}}$$

Once your costs per unit and selling price are known, you can calculate the break-even point, or the number of units that will need to be sold to cover your costs. This information can then be used for a number of key decisions such as whether to continue development of the product, whether to alter the price, what level of discount or special offers are affordable, whether to change suppliers in order to reduce costs, and so on.

Further techniques for improving profitability

There are several techniques that the entrepreneurial manager can employ to increase profits, and these are based on an understanding of the business finances. They include:

- focusing sales and advertising activities on those products and services that produce the best marginal, or gross, profit (if feasible, sales incentives can help achieve this);
- taking action on the less profitable products by reducing their cost, increasing price, reducing discount, or modifying the product so that it can command a higher sales price;
- ensuring that new products maintain or improve the business's overall profit margin.

Using financial ratios to manage profitability

Financial ratios are used by businesses to assess their performance, and ratios are also a valuable means of interpreting accounts. A ratio is simply a relationship between two numbers, but when compared to the same ratios for previous periods they can show important trends and patterns in performance. They are also useful for:

- benchmarking performance with other businesses in the same sector
- highlighting trends and identifying problems.

It should be remembered that ratios rely on accurate and consistent information.

Profitability ratios

Profitability ratios show how profitable the business is, and how good an investment it is as a result. One of the most important (and most often used) is the *gross profit margin*.

$$\text{Gross profit margin} = \frac{\text{gross profit}}{\text{sales}} \times 100$$

This ratio highlights the relationship between revenue (and its components of volumes and prices) with costs of sale. Similarly, the *net profit margin* examines the relationship between revenue and all other costs.

$$\text{Net profit margin} = \frac{\text{net profit}}{\text{sales}} \times 100$$

Return on capital employed (ROCE) is a ratio that will interest current and potential shareholders, and bankers, as it gives a comparison with what could have been achieved had the same amount of money been invested elsewhere.

$$ROCE = \frac{sales}{total\ capital\ employed} \times net\ profit\ per\ cent$$

Efficiency ratios

These are ratios that indicate how good the financial management is, as they highlight how quickly outstanding debts are collected; how quickly your business pays its debts, and how much working capital is tied up.

$$Average\ debtor\ collection\ period = \frac{365 \times debtors\ (amount\ owed\ to\ your\ business)}{sales}$$

This ratio is particularly important for managing cash flow and ensuring that the collection period is as short as possible. *Average payment period* can be calculated in a similar way, substituting creditors for debtors and costs of sales for sales.

Another important ratio for manufacturing and retailing businesses is *stock turnover*, as it can indicate the presence of slow moving stock, or too much stock that is hampering cash flow.

$$Stock\ turnover\ ratio = \frac{cost\ of\ sales}{stock\ level}$$

Liquidity ratios

Liquidity ratios show the business's ability to meet liabilities with the assets available. Of these, one of the most significant is the *current ratio:*

$$Current\ ratio = \frac{current\ assets}{current\ liabilities}$$

This ratio should normally be between 1.5 and 2; if it is less than 1, then current liabilities exceed current assets, and the business could be insolvent. For some industries it should be over 2 on the grounds that half the assets might be stock.

A more rigorous test of liquidity is the *quick ratio* or *acid test*. This takes into account the fact that some current assets, such as stock or work in progress, may be difficult to turn into cash quickly; deducting these from the current assets gives the quick assets.

$$Quick\ ratio\ (or\ acid\ test) = \frac{quick\ assets}{current\ liabilities}$$

The quick ratio is normally between 0.7 and 1; if the quick ratio is 1 or more, then quick assets exceed current liabilities and the business is safe. (Note: if the current ratio is rising and the quick ratio is largely unchanged then there is almost certainly a stockholding problem.)

Solvency ratios

Solvency ratios are similar to liquidity ratios in that they measure the ability of the business to meet its liabilities. However, whereas liquidity ratios show the *immediate* ability of the business to meet its liabilities, the solvency ratios show the *total* ability of the business to meet its debts (i.e. even if all the assets were sold and the business closed, would it be able to pay its debts?). One of the most common and important solvency ratios is the gearing (or ratio of debt to total finance).

$$Gearing = \frac{loans + bank\ overdraft}{equity + loans + bank\ overdraft}$$

There are several points to note about gearing:

- the higher the proportion of loan finance, then the higher the gearing;
- the gearing should not generally be greater than 50 per cent (although for new and small businesses it often is);
- if cash flow and profits are well established and secure, then the business can normally afford a higher gearing.

Checklist – techniques to increase profitability

There are many factors that affect profitability and cash flow. The leader should therefore consider focusing on some, or all, of the following issues. (Note that whilst one department or business function may have responsibility for one area, each function should work closely with each other to ensure profitability, viable cash flow and success.)

Reduce costs by examining attitudes

- Employees' attitudes to cost and wastage.
- Management's attitudes to cost control and reduction, and their understanding of the effects of expenses on cash flow *and* profitability.
- Attitudes to developing, monitoring and controlling budgets. Are they clearly understood and accepted, and do people feel ownership and responsibility for their budgets?

Production issues affecting profitability

- Suppliers and the business's buying policy. This can include the number

MANAGING FINANCE AND PROFITABILITY

of suppliers, the level of returns, the frequency that quotations are obtained, the availability and use of discounts.
- Number of overseas suppliers used and exchange rate implications.
- Quality processes and reducing waste.
- Customer returns and complaints.
- Amount and value of work in progress.
- Manufacturing and distribution lead-times.
- Costs of components and raw materials.
- Stock levels and mix, and stock control processes.
- Customer returns and complaints (as with stock, this is often a sales responsibility).

Development issues affecting profitability (particularly in the medium and long term)

- Costs of research and development (remember that too little may ultimately bring a bigger cost than too much, the key is therefore to know over what period do you want profitability to increase more: this month, or over the next three years?).
- Stage of product life cycle and the age (and value) of the product.

Sales and customer issues affecting profitability

- Sales expenses (e.g. travel costs per sales person).
- Market sectors that are served.
- The level of prospecting, i.e. the number of leads generated, customers served and revenue or profit generated per sales employee.
- Marketing and advertising response rates and marketing effectiveness.
- Image, reputation and quality of the business.
- Level of customer satisfaction.
- Levels of repeat business from existing customers.
- Pricing and discounts: are these *competitive*, *attractive* and *viable*?

People issues affecting profitability

- Whether staff feel they are fairly rewarded (whether they are or not can often be of secondary importance to whether they *feel* that they are being fairly rewarded).
- Staff training and levels of competence and expertise.
- Direction and management of personnel is vital for profitability. Do people know exactly what is expected of them, and have the necessary support to achieve their objectives?

Cash management issues

- Time taken to pay suppliers.
- The time that customers take to pay debts (i.e. the level of debtors and average age of accounts outstanding), and credit control policies and procedures.
- The number of bad debts: in particular their frequency and severity.

This is by no means an exhaustive list. Every business will have its own issues affecting its profitability and success, and these will be influenced by:

- *the type of industry,* e.g. service or manufacturing
- *the type of business* (the issues that a law firm may face will obviously differ from another service business such as an advertising agency)
- *the maturity of the business and the stage in development that it has reached,* e.g. a business start-up or a major multinational
- *the culture of the business* and the views and attitudes of its stakeholders (e.g. staff, suppliers, customers, shareholders)
- *the external environment,* e.g. whether there are conditions of economic prosperity or recession.

Summary: *Avoiding the pitfalls of financial management*

There are many financial pitfalls that the leader should be aware of, and these are the reasons why finance must be actively managed and led, rather than being left and neglected:

1. *Financial decisions are made in isolation,* without considering their impact on other departments, the business strategy and direction, cash management, or the realities of the market.
2. *Only the finance managers make financial plans and decisions.* Clearly everyone in the business needs to understand the importance of careful financial management for profitability and success; people need to feel ownership of their part of the process of financial control, and they need to have the information and expertise to routinely make the best financial decisions.

3. *Budgeting and budgetary control is poor.* Either budgets are used just to assess performance, rather than as an active tool to inform key financial decisions; or else budgets are cut across the board without regard to the business strategy and objectives *and how these will be achieved in practice.*
4. *Cash flow is unplanned* – with the result that the business is insolvent and dies, or alternatively cash is hoarded without reason when it could be invested, to the long-term detriment of the business.

As this section has highlighted, the dangers of simply leaving the business's finances to look after themselves are considerable, and financial leadership should be viewed as an essential aspect of overall commercial leadership.

Further information

Financial Control for Non-Financial Managers
D. Irwin, FT/Pitman, 1995

Accounts Demystified
A. Rice, FT/Pitman, 1993

Key Management Ratios
C. Walsh, FT/Pitman, 1993

Investment Appraisal
G. Mott, M&E Handbooks, 1993

Mentoring and coaching

Introduction

Mentoring can be defined as a process where the leader offers help, guidance and support to facilitate the learning or understanding of another. Mentoring is a key skill when delegating and also for a broad range of other management situations, including team-building, developing people, and managing change.

The four key qualities of mentors

There are many aspects to successful mentoring but four key qualities are widely recognised as being of special importance:

1. *Relevant work experience* – this includes passing on experience and knowledge of how best to approach the task, and where potential pitfalls lie.
2. *Experience and knowledge of the organisation* – knowing how to get things done and acting as a gateway to sources of information and support.
3. *Interpersonal skills* – knowing how to listen to others; asking questions that are both challenging and reflective. It is this 'sounding board' approach that is one of the most valuable aspects of mentoring and it is essential when getting a team member to focus on their task – how to approach it generally and how to solve problems.
4. *Role model* – providing an example that encourages, motivates and reassures the team member, making it clear that the task they are trying to achive is attainable.

Pitfalls for mentors

Inevitably, the qualities of a poor mentor are the same as those of a poor delegator:

- wishing to dominate and prescribing solutions;
- being critical and inflexible;
- being insensitive and authoritarian – for example, imposing solutions, plans and arbitrary deadlines;

- rigidly defending the status quo;
- talking, not listening.

These pitfalls can often result from insecurity. Also, some of these attitudes may result from a fear of change, and this, too, is nothing to be worried about. The answer is to focus on the needs of the task and the individual – what will it take to get the job done? Remember, change and innovation are the only ways to make progress.

Checklist – skills for effective mentoring

The skills and qualities needed for effective mentoring vary according to the aims and objectives of the mentoring process, and the approach taken to meet them. However, there are several approaches to mentoring that can be used, either separately or in combination.

Mentor qualities

Mentors need to have the following skills and qualities in order to be fully effective:

1. *Relevant work experience* is a vital element for successful mentoring. This does not mean that mentors need necessarily be tutors, nor does it require mentors to be experts in a particular topic, but mentors do need to have an understanding of what the learner is trying to achieve.
2. *Management perspective*, meaning that the mentor is either an experienced and competent manager, or alternatively has had exposure to management skills by working with managers. What is important is that the mentor has some understanding of management practice, pressures and techniques (e.g. delegation, team-building, time management, problem-solving, etc.).
3. *Credibility and 'organisational know-how'* are important as the mentor needs to enjoy personal and professional credibility within the organisation in order to get things done and support their learner, and they need to understand the system in which the learner works.
4. *Accessibility* – meaning that the mentor is prepared to make themselves available to their learners when the need arises.
5. *Communication and good interpersonal skills* – the mentor needs to be able to get the best out of their learner, building trust and helping them to develop their full potential. The mentor also needs to be sensitive and able to understand the learner's ideas, views and feelings. Of all the interpersonal skills, the core skills needed here are probably questioning and active listening (see COMMUNICATION SKILLS).
6. *An empowering approach* that has clear belief in the abilities of their

learner is necessary from a mentor. The mentor needs to be able to create the conditions for the learner to grow, try out new skills and methods, and make a greater contribution to the organisation.
7. *Creative and innovative* – the mentor must be open to new ideas, inventive and be able to consider (and even to suggest) new ways of doing things or approaching problems or issues. The mentor ideally needs to be able to perceive different and useful connections and patterns, and be a creative problem-solver in their own right.
8. *A focus on personal development* is an important quality for a mentor; the person should have experience of, and support for, the development of others.

Approaches to mentoring

- *Informal mentoring* – this occurs all the time and is an integral part of managing and leading people, whether planned or not. It occurs when trust is built up and a learner finds a more experienced colleague that they respect, trust and feel they can learn from.
- *Role model* – as a consequence of the mentoring process the learner will inevitably be influenced by the mentor's attitudes, values, problem-solving techniques and people management skills.
- *Sponsorship mentoring* – under this system the mentor provides a wide variety of experiences and opportunities for the learner, usually through special projects and assignments. This system is particularly useful in large organisations that may want to 'fast track' the development of key personnel or groups.
- *Peer group mentoring* – this system is most commonly used for new recruits joining an organisation, and it involves a responsible colleague at a similar level passing on their advice and help. It is an approach that works well as part of an induction process, and it is particularly useful for smaller organisations where training and development is achieved by using existing staff resources.

Implementing mentoring schemes

There are a number of fundamental reasons why leaders introduce mentoring schemes into organisations, including a desire to support and encourage individuals, develop confidence, spread expertise, promote professional development, implement change, raise morale and improve overall efficiency. Whatever the reason, the following factors are critical for the success of mentoring schemes:

- a supportive culture and work environment;
- visible top management commitment and support;

- participants are volunteers, and selection is rigorous;
- the mentoring scheme should have specific objectives and a limited time frame;
- agreed terms of reference and ongoing support is present for mentors;
- that the scheme is carefully monitored and regularly evaluated.

Most successful schemes start with the appointment of a champion who will plan, co-ordinate and implement the mentoring scheme. This individual needs to have a high level of interpersonal skill, organisational ability and enthusiasm. The champion needs to ensure that there is real and visible support from top management levels, and agree the purpose and aims of the mentoring scheme. The next step is to provide training and development for all mentors involved in the scheme. There also needs to be clear terms of reference in order to meet the individual and organisational objectives of the scheme. The terms of reference will differ between schemes but issues that should be considered include:

- *Confidentiality* – who gets to hear what? Should mentors discuss issues that learners have brought up with others, and if so what are the restrictions on this?
- *Communication* – how can mentors communicate with each other to examine common issues and problems?
- *Timetable* – what is expected of mentors, and when? How often should learners meet with mentors?
- *Support* – what should mentors do if things go wrong? Who should they contact?
- *Responsibilities* – where do responsibilities lie between mentor, learner, line manager, scheme sponsor?

Checklist – implementing mentoring schemes

Listed below are the critical issues that the mentoring scheme champion will need to resolve on the way to implementing a successful mentoring programme. The leader's responses to these questions, together with the other information from this section, should enable you to plan the implementation of a programme within your organisation.

- Would a mentoring scheme work in this organisation?
- Are there specific goals for the scheme?
- Have all the people that need to be involved been identified?
- How will the scheme be evaluated?
- Is there commitment from top management?
- How is this commitment expressed?
- Are all the necessary resources present?
- How will potential mentors be identified, approached and trained?

- How will mentors and learners be paired?
- Are there clear terms of reference and established guidelines for the scheme, and have these been clearly (and widely) communicated?
- What will happen if a problem occurs in a mentoring relationship?
- How will mentors be supported? What is the process and who needs to be involved?

Mentoring and coaching in practice

Mentoring has much in common with coaching, and coaching has a great deal to do with counselling. All three are about supporting an individual to overcome problems, achieve success and realise their full potential. For what it's worth, coaching focuses on the development of technique or a skill in a person by someone who is already skilled, and counselling is concerned with helping an individual resolve certain problems that they may be facing. I view them both as vital components of mentoring as a whole. Common skills for mentors, coaches and counsellors are strong interpersonal skills, and include:

- good listening skills
- good questioning – getting the learner to open up by asking open questions and avoiding yes or no answers
- suspending judgement
- giving constructive feedback
- checking understanding
- providing focus.

The value of all these attributes is that they:

- clarify issues
- solve problems
- create options
- change patterns of behaviour, enabling the individual to learn
- develop action plans to ensure that progress is made.

Both coaching and counselling rely on the agenda being set by the learner. Furthermore, the learner should discover their own way forward, and should feel commitment to their course of action because they have been the one responsible for establishing it. A mentor will be a *coach* because they help their learners develop the skills, attitudes, knowledge and understanding required to succeed at work. Mentors will be *counselling* when they are helping the learner deal with the wider problems and issues that they will inevitably face in their development. All three qualities – coaching, counselling and mentoring – are therefore vital elements for the successful leader to master.

Coaching effectively – the GROW model

Coaching can be seen as having four main phases:

1. Set *goals* both for the overall coaching relationship and for the individual session.
2. Explore the current position of the learner: the *reality* of their circumstances and their concerns.
3. Generate strategies, action plans and *options* for achieving the goals outlined above.
4. Decide *what* is to be done, by whom, how and when.

This is aptly known as the GROW model, and the central element is that responsibility for setting the goals ultimately rests with the learner. Goals set by others are more likely to be wrong, inappropriate, set too high or low and lack the commitment of the learner. The main objective of the mentor or coach is to *help the learner through this process*, chiefly by using effective questioning, rather than by instruction or reminiscing. The goals established should cover both the long term – what the learner hopes to achieve in the next twelve months with the coach/mentor's support – and the immediate purpose of the coaching/mentoring session, i.e. what can be achieved in the next half an hour or so.

Goal-setting

The quality of goal-setting is vital for successful coaching and mentoring, and goals should be SMART (like GROW this is another acronym): Specific, Measurable, Assignable, Realistic/Relevant, Time-constrained. By being *specific* and *measurable* it is possible to evaluate and provide feedback on goals, a factor that considerably improves the likelihood of the learner remaining committed to achieving them. It is important that goals are *assignable* and people involved in the project clearly know where responsibilities lie. Setting *realistic* goals is often difficult as they need to be challenging but achievable. When goals are *time-constrained* this ensures that effort is focused on achieving them as there is a deadline to meet.

It is worth noting that, in general, the greater control and involvement that learners have in setting and achieving their goals, then the more likely they are to achieve success. Conversely, the greater the level of outside influences, changing circumstances or reliance on others, then the more likely it is that learners will fail to remain committed to their goals, seeing them as subject to circumstances largely beyond their control. An antidote to this frequent problem, besides encouraging the individual to examine the facts of the matter, suggest a solution and find another route to their objective, is to help distinguish between *end goals* and *performance goals*. End goals are the ultimate objective of a learner. They could typically be to gain promotion or additional responsibility, or complete a major project. Performance goals establish the level of performance that will help an individual to achieve their end goal. Performance goals include such elements as quality standards, time management and production targets.

Understanding the reality and options phases of the GROW model

The purpose of the reality phase is to enable the learner to analyse and understand their current situation quickly. This can include facts or figures, obstacles, resources available or people involved in the situation. The role of the coach or mentor is essentially to prompt the learner by asking questions that uncover the reality. The coach can also help by providing information, if possible, and also by summarising the situation so far, as this will help to clarify the reality for the learner.

The coach then needs to help the learner see the way forward, and this is done by *generating* and *selecting* options. The learner needs to feel comfortable with, and committed to the option they choose.

Deciding what is to be done – the final phase of the GROW model

Finally, the learner needs to generate a practical action plan so that they can implement their chosen option. The coach's role here is largely as a sounding board, highlighting strengths and weaknesses and offering an additional perspective that supports the learner. The plan needs to include the what, when, who and how elements; ideally a review and feedback process to check progress, and the necessary resources and attitude to ensure success. The coach's role is to help provide these and encourage the learner to use them.

Questions for coaches and mentors to ask

There are many questions that coaches can ask to support the learner and focus the coaching process. The same questions can also be used for self-coaching – all you need to do is consider a major issue at work that you would like to resolve.

- What are you trying to achieve?
- How will you know when you have achieved it?
- Would you define it as an *end goal* or a *performance goal*?
- If it is an end goal, what performance goal could be related to it?
- Is the goal specific?
- In what way is it measurable?
- To what extent can you control the result, what sort of things won't you have control over?
- Do you feel that achieving the goal will stretch or break you?

- When do you want to achieve the goal by?
- What are the milestones or key points on the way to achieving your goal?
- Who is involved and what effect could they have on the situation?
- What have you done about this situation so far, and what have been the results?
- What are the major constraints in finding a way forward?
- Are these constraints major or minor? How could their effect be reduced?
- What other issues are occurring at work that might have a bearing on your goal?
- What options do you have?
- If you had unlimited resources what options would you have?
- Could you link your goal to some other organisational issue?
- What would be the perfect solution?

Once the learner has assessed their position the time comes to select the best option and take action. The following questions may then be useful:

- What are you going to do?
- When are you going to do it?
- Who needs to know?
- What support and resources do you need, and how will you get them?
- How will the above help you to achieve your goals?
- What obstacles might hinder you and what strategies do you have for countering these?

Summary: *Starting to mentor*

The following guidelines may prove useful for the first mentoring session:

- Establish overall goals for mentoring, through questioning and feedback.
- Explore the current situation and establish expectations.
- Establish a selection of strategies to achieve goals, including how the mentor and learner will work together.
- Evaluate strategies and select.
- Establish written agreement on the next steps, noted as a formal action plan.

Subsequent sessions should include feedback and evaluation of the previous sessions, goals and planning. Goals should always be set first to establish an agenda for the session.

Further information

The Mentoring Manager
G. Lewis, FT/Pitman, 1995

Successful Mentoring in a Week
G. Lewis and S. Carter, Hodder Headline, 1995

Mentoring (Managing Best Practice)
Industrial Society, 1995

Coaching and Mentoring
N. MacLennan, Gower, 1995

Coaching for Performance: A practical guide to growing your own skills
J. Whitemore, Nicholas Brealey, 1995

Motivation and empowerment

> **Introduction**
>
> Motivation and empowerment are two of the defining, core skills of leadership, and they are included together as they are both about getting the best from people. These two skills are a vital, underpinning factor in virtually everything that the leader does – from delegation to decision-making – as well as being skills that need to be developed in their own right. Although they share a great deal in common with each other, such as a positive and sensitive approach, there are also some key techniques that are different for each skill.

Motivating people

> *50 per cent of motivation comes from within a person, and 50 per cent from his or her environment, especially from the leadership encountered therein.*
> (From *Effective Motivation* by John Adair)

Introduction

Undoubtedly people are motivated by a complex array of different factors; so, for example, the 'carrot and stick' approach is only one of many motives governing action. An alternative approach is the more cynical 'stimulus–response' view of *expectancy theory*, whereby behaviour rests on the instinctive tendency for individuals to balance the value of expected benefits against the expenditure of energy. While this may occasionally be applicable for certain people or in certain situations, it is an extreme view that does not do justice to the vast majority of peoples' motivations. For example, people may be highly motivated by money, but they are not *only* or even *always* motivated by money.

An individual's strength of motivation is affected by the expectations of outcomes from certain actions, but it is also strengthened by other factors such as the individual's preferred outcome; conditions in the working environment, as well as the individual's perceptions and fears.

Factors affecting motivation

Motivation is a varied and complex skill and leaders often fail because they do not understand just how difficult and complex it is. Three factors affecting the leader's success at motivation are:

- *Understanding what motivates an individual to act* – this is fundamental to engaging that person and focusing their efforts. Motives are inner needs or desires and these can be conscious, semi-conscious or subconscious. Motives can also be mixed, with several clustered around a primary motive.
- *Understanding the external environment* – different influences, such as the needs of the team or the desire to avoid a difficult situation later, often need to be understood by the leader.
- *The role of the leader,* who must themselves be completely self-motivated, is also a key element in motivating others.

Eight rules for leaders when motivating people

1. Be motivated yourself

Leadership requires self-motivation in order to:

- set a clear example of the level of effort, commitment and purpose – motivation – that is required from subordinates;
- fully understand the causes of motivation in each situation;
- drive progress forward, overcoming any obstacles (this is why motivation is important generally, for the leader *and* the team).

2. Select people who are highly motivated

Understanding individual's motivation starts right at the beginning of the selection interview. People may often be motivated, but their motivation needs to be *appropriate to the requirements of the job*. For example, not everybody is motivated to sell or become a sales person, their motivation lies elsewhere.

3. Treat each person as an individual

When motivating, it is often wrong to assume that everyone will respond in the same way to the same stimulus or promise. Indeed, people may often react *against* being viewed the same as others. Everyone will have their own feelings resulting from individual perspectives, experiences and personality, and these will affect their motivation. The more the leader understands what motivates someone, the more success they will have in focusing that person. (Treating people as individuals is also vital for empowerment: there needs to be an understanding of the person's views and feelings, and how much responsibility they can take on.)

4. Set realistic and challenging targets

When leading people it is often easy to set targets that are too difficult and unattainable for the individual, resulting in failure and demotivation. The other side of the coin is to set targets that are just too easy, and while this may occasionally be desirable to give a boost to the person there are the dangers that:

- the real work is not being done as quickly as possible;
- the person may feel patronised and demotivated;
- when harder targets are needed the person has not developed sufficiently to succeed with them.

The trick is therefore to understand the needs of the team, task and individual and set targets that are challenging but realistic. This provides a focus for the individual to channel their efforts and ensures a sense of purpose.

5. Remember that progress motivates

Achieving success is a great motivator, and because of this the best teams often celebrate their successes. There is a virtuous spiral that occurs when success is achieved as it reinforces confidence and motivation, and this in turn generates further success.

6. Create a motivating environment

The leader has to create the right conditions in which people can thrive and this means:

- ensuring that there are no structural obstacles (such as needless bureaucracy, policies or procedures) that can hamper the individual and reduce motivation;
- making sure that the individual is not frustrated by a lack of necessary resources;
- understanding any training and development needs;
- monitoring progress – coaching and guiding where necessary – and acknowledging achievements.

7. Provide fair rewards

Rewards are a form of recognition and are important in maintaining motivation; they can congratulate as well as encourage and can take a number of forms, for example, promotion, additional resources or extra responsibilities, as well as pay and benefits.

8. Give recognition

Recognition of successes achieved or effort involved will go a long way to ensuring that the team member's motivation is sustained. The leader needs to maintain their team member's momentum for their ongoing success.

What people look for in a job

Research by the Policy Studies Institute in the UK has identified an interesting list of factors that people look for in a job:

Enjoying the work	84%
Job security	83%
A good relationship with the supervisor	80%
Potential to use their abilities	78%
Able to use their initiative	75%
Friendly people to work with	74%
Good training provision	72%
Good pay	71%
Good physical working conditions	70%

(Source: *Employee Commitment and The Skills Revolution*, Policy Studies Institute)

The same research also provided a list of the top reasons *why* people go to work:

	Men	*Women*
Earning money to pay for essentials	76%	53%
Job satisfaction	51%	56%
Because of the company of work colleagues	23%	46%
Following a career	33%	28%

Empowerment

Empowerment takes motivation and delegation one step further: it is a way of releasing the creative power that a team has, not for one specific task but in their job as a whole. It is based on the belief that the full capabilities of team members are frequently under-used, and given the right work environment and level of responsibility people will start to make a much greater, positive contribution. In effect, when empowering team members you are letting them get on with the job *entirely*: they are both responsible and accountable, within certain agreed boundaries.

Empowerment is about:

- Letting each member of the team get on with their job.
- Letting those team members closest to customers (both within and outside the organisation) take decisions themselves.
- Removing obstacles and unnecessary bureaucracy.

- Encouraging and enabling people to put their ideas for improvement into practice.

Key stages in empowering your team

1. *Understand what you mean by empowerment* – make sure you know what you want to get out of empowering your team; let your colleagues and senior managers know your plans, and check that their expectations meet your own.
2. *Assess the barriers to empowerment* – what are they (for example, staff may fear responsibility, or there may be a bureaucratic or conservative culture that is unreceptive to change), and how can they be overcome?
3. *Build the right culture within your team* – some organisations have cultures that are more conducive to empowerment than others. If you are serious about empowering your team to make their own decisions and take greater responsibility, then you should promote trust and respect; remove a climate of fear and blame, and focus on the needs of the task, team and each individual.
4. *Establish the boundaries* – empowerment provides staff with greater autonomy and responsibility, but it is important that you agree and set clear limits. This may include referring types of decision, such as agreeing expenditure above a certain level, to you. Also, be prepared to have these boundaries tested: only then will clear limits be established.
5. *Communicate and win support* – you will need to raise awareness among those around you of what is involved in empowerment: this may involve reassuring some, selling the benefits and winning the support of others.
6. *Ensure that your staff have the necessary skills and resources to take control* – review what each member of your team does now and what they are likely to be doing in future. This is an opportunity to alter and update job descriptions; assess training needs, and make sure that your team has sufficient resources.
7. *Agree objectives and performance measures* – empowerment is about giving people the responsibility and resources to complete tasks on an ongoing basis. As with delegation, it is not about dumping work on people and leaving them, and it requires you to agree the necessary level of speed, accuracy and cost-efficiency.
8. *Launch and support the empowerment initiative, and monitor developments* – once the ground has been prepared empowerment can take effect. You will need to make people aware of what is happening and try to secure early 'wins' and successes that highlight the value of the process. Monitor developments and iron out any difficulties, particularly in the

early days, but be sure that you are not interfering or undermining the process!

It is important to understand that when you empower your team members you are giving them a complete *job* and area of responsibility, within definite boundaries, rather than delegating one specific *task or project*.

> **Summary:** *Essentials of empowerment*
>
> Empowering people requires the leader to:
>
> - Set a clear, unambiguous direction and ensure that people remain on course.
> - Retain a full understanding of what is happening.
> - Offer support, open doors, and clear the way for action without taking over from those delegated to do the job.
> - Make decisions which others cannot, either because of lack of time, information or knowledge.
> - Continuously assess performance, reward progress, and support individual and team development.
> - Build trust through shared success and share information and knowledge whenever it is possible to do so.

Further information

Empowering People
A.M. Stewart, FT/Pitman, 1994

Handbook of Management
D. Lock (Editor), Gower, 1995

Finding and Keeping the Right People
J. Billsberry, FT/Pitman, 1996

Handbook of Personnel Management Practice
M. Armstrong, Kogan Page, 1996

Managing Difficult Staff
H. Drummond, Kogan Page, 1980

Empowered Teams
R. Wellins, W. Byham and J. Wilson, Jossey Bass, 1991

Negotiating skills

Introduction

Negotiating is one of the most frequently used leadership skills: vital to achieving success, it still provokes a wide range of conflicting views and approaches. Traditional views of the art of negotiating have tended to emphasise the need to enforce one's will on the negotiation, which itself is seen as an adversarial process or a battle between two forces with clear winners and losers. This view emphasises the importance of strength and toughness – even deceit – to grind the other party down and eventually triumph. However, in recent years negotiations have become increasingly complex and the costs of failure, either during the negotiation or after, have risen significantly. This has resulted in a more sensitive, practical and realistic approach to negotiating. The 'new' approaches emphasise the need to reach a consensus, *a 'win–win' agreement that is to the mutual benefit of all parties*. Only by reaching an agreement that is acceptable on all sides will the outcome be fair, providing lasting benefit and preventing the need to renegotiate or abrogate the agreement in the future.

The advantages of win–win agreements

Negotiating within a framework of trust, principles and respect promotes short-term strength and success, as well as fostering better long-term relationships. There are many advantages to conducting negotiations honestly, openly and seeking to reach a win–win agreement that provides mutual benefit, including:

Universally understood and welcome

Honesty and openness are qualities that are universally understood and appreciated. You do not need to understand the other person's background or character to know that the right thing to do is to show respect for their position and to be honest. In most cases people will respond favourably, which will help to ensure that the negotiation is positive and ultimately successful.

Strengthen your own position

Laying the ground-rules and leading by example not only helps to remove you from any blame should the negotiation fail, but it positively strengthens your case from the start, giving the initiative to the leader that takes this approach.

Engender trust and co-operation

There are many instances when the negotiator will actually achieve *more* concessions from the party that they are negotiating with by taking a win–win approach. This is because it can help significantly in engendering trust: the other party may then be more constructive in their approach, or simply more inclined to accommodate the view of someone that they trust.

Reach better agreements that endure

Win–win also ensures that both parties are satisfied with the outcome. As a result, there is a more positive approach to making the agreement work, as there is no lingering resentment or bitterness. In objective terms the agreement is also more likely to work if it meets the needs of both parties.

However, there are exceptional circumstances when win–win is not a desirable outcome, and the result must be win–lose. The most obvious examples are negotiations with terrorists and criminals, but even within the normal work environment there are times when certain types of behaviour must be stopped, or situations reversed, permanently. These tend to be rather uncommon, but none the less the leader needs to realise when the only outcome that is acceptable is win–lose, and the offender needs to understand the sanction that will follow if the agreement is broken. These types of agreement are usually less satisfactory and more fragile than win–win, and need closer monitoring, but they may be unavoidable.

Checklist – preparing to negotiate

Thorough preparation is an essential part of negotiating successfully; unfortunately it is frequently overlooked with the resulting danger that the agreement will be made quickly and rashly. Preparing to negotiate should usually involve most, if not all, of the following elements.

Know when a negotiation is taking place

Many people negotiate without even realising it! They set out their position, discuss the other parties' concerns and reach an agreement, yet because they did not realise that they were negotiating it may prove to be an unsatisfactory outcome. They may well have been unprepared, failing to explore all options, and as a result may feel resentful or pressured afterwards – or possibly just plain dissatisfied with the outcome. This typically happens in dealings with staff when, for example, assigning a task can turn into a negotiation between the outcome that the leader wants and that desired by their colleague. Another example is during a selling process, where the salesman moves seamlessly from *describing* their product or service to getting you to *accept* it, without even the barest hint of a negotiation along the way! Knowing *when* you are in a negotiation is as important as knowing *what you want* the outcome to be.

Ensure that you are in the right frame of mind

To reach the best possible agreement you must be in the right frame of mind, typically avoiding tiredness or emotional behaviour that will cause distractions or generally hinder your effectiveness. The right frame of mind means that you should:

- want to reach a settlement or solution;
- think in terms of finding a common solution, rather than unremittingly pursuing your own agenda;
- be open-minded, positive and flexible in your aims – always look for the answer;
- be calm, so that your judgement is clear and unimpaired;
- be sensitive to the other side – what matters to them and what does not;
- consider establishing trust and a rapport as one way of reaching a constructive settlement.

Have a clear understanding of all of the key issues

Good negotiators should explore *all* possible avenues and their consequences for the parties *before* committing to a particular outcome. This helps to prevent more attractive alternative situations being discovered later that can result in one or more of the parties reneging on the agreement. To do this successfully the negotiator therefore needs to understand at least the *essentials* of the matter under discussion. However, a word of warning. Too much detail, particularly in complex issues, can lead to both parties focusing on smaller matters (precisely because it is so complex and absorbing), rather than stepping back, seeing the bigger picture and then reaching an agreement. Sometimes complex negotiations can be like walking continually around the woods without ever seeing daylight. In these situations a thorough understanding of the core issues will enable you to get back to first principles – and find your way to an agreement from there.

Know yourself: the aims, strengths and weaknesses of your position and approach

It is important when preparing that you are clear about your aims – the outcome that you would favour. This will highlight areas where you can concede and where you cannot. It is also important that you understand the strengths and weaknesses of your position; in this way you can be clear about what to do if they attack your weak spot *before they do*, rather than find yourself taken by surprise. You should also be clear about the tactics that you will use to achieve your aims, and you should agree with the others on your side what the best approach would be.

Know the other party

Understanding the objectives of the other parties involved in the negotiation is also vital. It will help you to assess what is important to them, and where the possible areas for compromise lie.

Develop a clear, workable strategy

Clearly understanding your own aims, interests and motivations – as well as those of the other party – will help you in developing a strategy for the negotiation. The key questions are: What do you want, and how might you achieve it? You will then be better able to identify areas of common interest and areas of potential conflict for all sides, and then explore possible solutions. In preparing, you should, therefore:

- be clear about what you hope to achieve;
- know your own strengths and weaknesses;
- be ready to explore possible solutions to areas of conflict;
- be ready to explore ways to use and promote areas of common interest to facilitate an agreement;
- establish points upon which you do not wish to concede. Be clear why they are important and adhere to them consistently;
- be prepared to seek additional expert advice – particularly if you are unfamiliar with the subject in question.

Select and prepare the team

The team that you choose will reflect the subject matter, goals and type of negotiation. It is important to:

- decide how many people will be involved;
- choose people with the appropriate skills, expertise and character for the negotiation;

- decide each team member's area of responsibility, and allow them to focus their skills on a particular function;
- if necessary, appoint a leader who can co-ordinate the team, inspire confidence and trust, communicate well and conduct the negotiations according to a pre-planned strategy and style;
- ensure that team members understand and support your aims and approach;
- ensure that team members understand pre-planned signals that communicate thoughts and messages, such as a concern over a point and a desire to discuss the issue privately. After all, you may not wish to alert the other side to particular concerns until you have had a chance to explore them yourself.

Be clear about the arrangements for the negotiation

It may seem obvious and even trivial, but knowing the arrangements for the negotiation (e.g. venue, timing and who will be present) can be important in ensuring that you are prepared and create the right impression. In many respects it is like a job interview: courtesy, effort and preparation all go a long way to creating a positive atmosphere, and making sure that you yourself are not rude, distracted or flustered.

Checklist – negotiating strategies and techniques

Listed below are the main techniques that negotiators will use, or at least encounter, during the negotiating process. The important aspects are to be prepared, focused on what you want to achieve, positive and confident, and comfortable. Every leader needs to develop their own negotiating style, and this will certainly include some of the following strategies and techniques.

Starting the negotiation and resolving problems

Starting the negotiation positively is clearly important. An agenda may help, and both sides might want to make a preliminary statement, but both sides certainly need to explain what they want to achieve. You might consider starting the negotiation by asking the other party about their position and what they wish to achieve, but if they refuse at this early stage then the next step is for you to outline your position in general terms, and then ask them to comment. In this way you will draw out their views and priorities.

Joint problem-solving in a negotiation is often a difficult task and each negotiator will have their own individual style. However, there are several key stages in the problem-solving process:

1. Clarify what you believe are the main issues under discussion. This

involves stating *why* you believe you are meeting and what you want jointly to achieve.
2. Ask the other participants what they want to achieve.
3. Ask for their opening position – what they see as the main issues.
4. State your opening position and clearly focus both parties on a positive outcome.

Communicate effectively

It is important when you speak that you are clear about the points you want to make and that you are focused on achieving a satisfactory final outcome. Details are included earlier in COMMUNICATION SKILLS, but the essentials when negotiating are:

- *Stop talking* – remember that *listening* is vital to communicating well.
- *Empathise* – try to put yourself in the other person's position so that you can understand and overcome their concerns, and keep their commitment to you and the task.
- *Be sensitive to their body language* – eye contact, mirroring body language and understanding what their posture means can all be important.
- *Question* – asking questions not only improves your understanding but it can also test assumptions and show that you are listening.
- *Summarise* – give an overview at the start of what you want to say, and finish by summarising what has been agreed. Summarising at key intervals also helps to prevent misunderstandings and move the conversation on to the next point.
- *Maintain professionalism and control emotions* – controlling your emotions is essential for staying focused on the issues and resolving the negotiation satisfactorily.
- *Maintain critical awareness* – this requires a variety of skills, in particular reacting to ideas, not people; focusing on the significance to the discussion of the facts and evidence; avoiding jumping to conclusions; listening for *how* things are said, and what is *not* said.
- *Avoid taking hasty decisions* – give yourself time to think and react.
- *Understand yourself* – recognise your own views and prejudices and avoid letting them influence your behaviour.
- *Be sensitive and tactful, and in difficult situations choose your words carefully* – remember, if you disagree with what is being said don't start by saying that you disagree: this can often prompt a defensive or negative response. Instead, outline your views first and then explain why you disagree.

NEGOTIATING SKILLS

Case studies: *1. The importance of preparation;*
2. Techniques for cross-cultural negotiating

A lawyer with a major London law firm, who was a very successful negotiator, told me two stories about his experience as a negotiator.

The first concerned a meeting he was having in New York. He was representing his client in contractual negotiations with a firm that wanted to supply his client with computer hardware, software and systems support. He did his homework and spoke to other lawyers and people in the industry about the company he was going to be dealing with. The message he got back was surprising: two people separately told him that the commercial director he would be dealing with had broken down in tears during the negotiation; the meeting had paused and one of her colleagues asked if they could accept some of their terms. Caught off guard, they had agreed and given more than they intended.

So forewarned, my friend went into battle and, sure enough, the commercial director broke into tears at a critical moment in the negotiation. My friend was unmoved, and although careful not to show anger he demanded to know whether the negotiation could continue, or whether they would prefer to travel to London and conclude business in his office. The tears soon stopped and an agreement was reached.

The second story concerned a negotiation between a major European retailer and a team of Chinese government officials. The retailer wanted to set up a business in China and the lawyer was handling the arrangements. Again, my friend had prepared considerably in advance of the meeting and knew what to expect. The Chinese business culture in general and approach to negotiating in particular are very different from that normally encountered in the West, and the following points were invaluable:

1. *Keep an emotional distance* – when negotiating in a

different culture it is often easy to judge anything new as bad, rather than just different.
2. *Check assumptions* as part of the pre-negotiation preparation.
3. *Understand what matters to the other side* – in the case of the Chinese culture, 'face' and respect are emphasised much more than in the West.
4. *Understand **who** holds power, and **how** decisions are made.* It is also important to understand Chinese respect for authority and influential people – and to use this to your advantage if necessary.
5. *Consider using an intermediary* (who may already have the confidence and respect of the other side, as well as valuable experience) – and use your own interpreter.
6. *Negotiate around 'regulations'* – government officials the world over often cite rules and regulations as a reason for disagreeing with things they do not like. The answer is to respect this but to look for a pragmatic solution that will conform with the regulations and still deliver a solution acceptable to both sides. This can be achieved by defining the issue and looking for alternatives.
7. *Allow enough time* – and make sure that you are not in a position where you can be pressured by time constraints.

Question

Questioning is an invaluable tool when negotiating; it is versatile, suiting most occasions, and it allows you to focus on the issue without having to be too confrontational. In particular it can be useful when you want:

- time to consider a proposal that someone has made
- to show interest or concern
- to clarify your understanding or if you need further information
- to test resolve and depth of feeling
- to calm someone down who is angry or emotional
- to make your point forcefully.

Many skilled negotiators are trained to use a questioning approach as a fallback response; it requires skill and is worth considering carefully.

Build agreement – getting to yes

With some negotiations it can be the case that a simple meeting of minds and discussion is enough to clear away the difficulties and reach an agreement. However, this tends to happen in simple and straightforward negotiations where the issues are few and clear-cut; more normally, there are many factors requiring agreement and in this situation there are two possible approaches:

1. *Build a consensus and reach agreement gradually, step-by-step* – this is necessary in some cultures, or when dealing with highly sensitive or complex issues, where the process tends to be a long series of minor negotiations.
2. *Take an overall (holistic) approach to the negotiation* – this can involve one of the parties making a major concession in order to reach a quick agreement; it can also mean presenting an overall plan for an agreement that provides a win–win solution, offering benefits for both parties.

Understand the importance of ownership

For a negotiation to succeed in the medium to long term, all parties must be able to enjoy some input and claim some success. Without ownership of the process and the final outcome, one party can be left uncommitted to the agreement, ultimately resulting in the undoing of that agreement.

Record what has been agreed

It is often useful to confirm points that have been agreed during the negotiating process – particularly for difficult or complex discussions. Record what is agreed, and confirm it in writing at the end.

Be prepared to handle impromptu negotiations (for example, on the telephone)

If you are being called, ask for an outline, but do not commit yourself to negotiating or deciding. By agreeing to return the call later you will give yourself some time to prepare thoroughly and enter negotiations at a time that suits you.

If you are calling, avoid potential interruptions and choose a suitable time. Having prepared for the most likely responses, follow your plan and know how you are going to deal with each eventuality.

It is also useful to summarise agreements and confirm in writing afterwards.

Take your time and think carefully

This does not mean that you are slow to react to every point – obviously there will be times, particularly when you feel strongly about something or if you already have a reply ready, when you will respond immediately. However, it is also important not to rush to fill empty silences and to give yourself some time to think carefully; to do this you could consider the following techniques:

- wait for the other person to finish making their point before making yours;
- reflect back on what has been said, checking understanding, clarifying their meaning and also testing their resolve;
- announce your pause, either with phrases such as 'That's an interesting point' or else simply by asking for time to think ('Well I will need to consider that point further').

Stay focused and objective – avoid becoming emotional

Some negotiators play on the personal behaviours of the people they are negotiating with to influence the final outcome in their favour. This might include using flattery, or alternatively using behaviours designed to upset the other person, such as being patronising or ridiculing them.

Avoid diluting your arguments

Many negotiators believe that presenting a large number of arguments will result in a landslide of 'evidence' and facts that will overwhelm the other party. In truth, this more usually *reduces* the effectiveness of your key points, by diluting them with the other less significant issues. A better approach used by skilled negotiators is to present a few (two or three) powerful arguments first, and then move down the list of arguments in descending order of effectiveness if those were unsuccessful. This can still counter the other party, without resulting in any points being lost or ineffective.

Negotiating concessions

Do not feel obliged to agree concessions immediately: instead, give yourself time to consider the point fully and how it relates to the overall negotiation.

Know when you would prefer to withdraw from the negotiations

Deciding upon situations in which you would prefer to withdraw is a technique that is often known as a *trip-wire*. Calling a halt to the negotiation does not automatically imply the end, but more usually a chance to reflect, regain perspective and prepare for the resumption of talks.

Be prepared to recognise and face failure

As a leader you should decide what options you will have if a negotiated settlement proves unattainable. (This approach, known as the *best alternative to a negotiated settlement* [BATNA], was first made explicit by Harvard Law School.) Research has highlighted the fact that knowing you have an alternative strategy allows you to negotiate from a position of confidence and strength.

Assessing offers when negotiating

You should have in mind three types of outcome when you prepare for the negotiation:

1. *Ideal* – the solution that best meets your needs
2. *Realistic* – the one that is most likely, possibly the fairest
3. *Fall-back* – the result that is at the limit of what you can accept.

Compare the offer (or deal) with your planned outcomes

When you assess offers you need to assess them against these three outcomes, and to find out where the offer fits there are several key questions that need to be answered and assessed:

- Is this the best deal that you can get at this stage? Is it a final offer? (Note: beware of the *false final offer*. Judge for yourself the real position by questioning and probing to find out how they arrived at their offer, precisely how it was calculated, and what would happen if you were unable to agree.)
- Is it a reasonable or win–win solution?
- How will others react to this offer?
- Are you being objective about the offer, or are you being unduly influenced by other factors (such as tiredness, urgency or your view of the people – good or bad – that you are negotiating with)?

Checking objectivity

An important means of checking objectivity and whether an offer is acceptable or not is to consider VIP: *Value, Implementation* and *Price*. This means asking further questions, either of yourself or the other party, so that you can best assess the offer.

- *Value* – how important is the concession or offer being made to you? Do you value it, and if so how much? Is it a part of the ideal, realistic or fallback solution?
- *Implementation* – how easy will this offer/deal/part of the deal be to

work in practice? It may sound fantastic but if it is unrealistic, unworkable or impractical then it is not important. It is also worth considering how easy it is to communicate and sell to others: even if you think it is a good and workable offer, will it be rendered impractical by the attitudes of others?

- *Price* – most offers come at a price: the negotiator needs to understand what is expected in return, and whether the price is fair and one worth paying. (This may not necessarily be a financial value.)

Avoiding pitfalls and ensuring success in negotiations

When negotiating you should avoid:

1. *Using provocative or irritating phrases,* either intentionally or unintentionally, or phrases that imply hidden meanings. For example, 'with respect' can be taken to mean the exact opposite, and 'I hear what you say' clearly implies 'I don't care what you think'. Also, certain phrases, such as 'you failed', 'you insisted' or 'you did not' should be used only infrequently, when you want to bring about direct confrontation.
2. *Issuing counter-proposals without even appearing to consider the other party's original proposal.* Few things will irritate or annoy as much as appearing to disregard a proposal or suggestion: discussing, probing and questioning it will reveal any limitations and highlight your concerns, enabling you to move on to your counter-proposal which then stands much more chance of getting a fair hearing.
3. *Engaging in criticism or the appearance of criticism.* Many remarks can be taken as criticism and the normal response is to fight back. The result is a spiral of attack followed by defence which is perceived as an attack, so there is another defence which is perceived as an attack, and so on. This destroys trust and understanding and can soon shatter any prospect of reaching a win–win settlement.

When negotiating you should consider applying the following techniques:

1. *Using behaviour labelling.* This is when you say what you are going to do before you do it, prefacing your remarks with words such as *'I'd like to make a point. I think that ...'* or *'I'd like to clarify something. What was the reason for...'* This focuses the other party's attention, gives you time to organise your thoughts and ensures that the other person is receptive and ready to respond.
2. *Being honest and constructive.* Taking this approach ensures that you get your message and concerns across clearly, but in a way that does criticise the other party, causing defensiveness or bad-feeling. (For example,

'Is there anything else that is relevant here?' is better than saying *'What are you hiding?'*)
3. *Testing understanding.* This ensures that you and everyone else understands the present position; it gives you the chance to state the issue in your own words, enabling people to view it from your perspective, and it slows things up, giving everyone time to think.
4. *Summarising.* Like testing understanding, summarising also provides a useful opportunity for everyone involved to think and reflect on where the negotiation has reached. *Mid-discussion summaries* in the course of the negotiation ensure that no issue that people thought was agreed is lost or misunderstood, and they provide a clear bridge from one point to the next. *Summarising agreement* is a chance for each party to write down the points that have been agreed and the decisions that have been made (it is also a useful tool at meetings too). It is also an important opportunity to prevent any misunderstanding. Summaries should ensure that no action or point is left ambivalent, and summaries should conclude the negotiation by:

- agreeing the action points from the meeting, and time-scales for their completion
- agreeing any items that were not resolved and what would happen with them (e.g. referred to others, discussed next time)
- agreeing the time, location and purpose of the next meeting.

Summary: *Negotiating successfully*

1. *Prepare* – know what you want and what you can offer, and decide on the best approach and tactics to reach a win–win settlement.
2. *Start positively* – begin with your view of what is being negotiated and then ask for the view of the others. Next ask for their opening position and state yours.
3. *Think carefully and take your time (avoid being rushed or 'bounced' into a situation)* – this means treating the other party as you would wish to be treated: letting them outline their arguments and giving them fair consideration. Do not be afraid to ask for time to think and reflect, and summarise as well – it helps to clarify understanding and also buys you time.
4. *Question and probe* – test their statements and consider what they say *and how they say it*. Getting all the information that you need to make a

decision is vitally important when negotiating, and can mean the difference between success and failure.

5. *Keep positive* – your approach needs to focus on the goal of reaching the best win–win solution available, and to do this you will almost certainly need to make concessions. When you discuss issues you should:

   – soften disagreements
   – avoid criticism, implying blame and either defensive or offensive postures
   – minimise emotional responses (either yours or theirs)
   – be prepared to explain your reasoning

6. *Use techniques that work for you and get the best from the other party* – this requires a range of factors; for example, testing understanding, using behaviour labelling, summarising, and avoiding diluting your argument.

7. *Assess offers rationally and objectively* – this means measuring offers against the ideal, realistic and fallback scenarios; checking the sincerity and finality of the offer, and assessing offers for their value, ease of implementation and price or cost to you.

Finally, it is also worth considering that any offers you make will probably be assessed in the same way!

Further information

One Stop Contracts
D. Martin and J. Wyborn, ICSA Publishing Ltd, 1996

Successful Negotiating in a Week
P. Fleming, Hodder Headline, 1993

How to Negotiate Worldwide – A practical handbook
D.W. Hendon and R.A. Hendon

Thinking on Your Feet in Negotiations
J. Hodgson, FT/Pitman, 1995

Effective Negotiating
C. Robinson, Kogan Page, 1996

The Language of Negotiation
J. Mulholland, Routledge, 1991

One Stop Negotiation
D. Martin, ICSA Publishing, 1997

Problem-solving

Introduction

The need to solve problems quickly and effectively arises throughout organisations and is closely related to decision-making. Both involve a logical and systematic approach to defining the problem, generating possible solutions, choosing and then implementing the best option. However, the hidden trap within problem-solving is the danger of *over-analysis*: often what is really required is nothing more than a pen, paper and a period of quiet thought and discussion. Just as there are leadership styles so there are problem-solving styles: methods or processes that successful leaders regularly rely on to resolve difficult issues. This section outlines a framework for successful problem-solving and each part of the process can be used in isolation – depending on the type of problem.

Also included is a short overview of the popular Myers Briggs type inventory, one of the most popular and enduring tools of the last fifty years for assessing different styles of problem analysis and decision-making.

Problem-solving process

There are a number of steps to follow – or to encourage your team to follow – when solving problems:

1. overcome barriers
2. define the problem
3. gather relevant information
4. identify possible causes
5. identify a possible solution
6. check the solution, consider other possible options
7. make the decision
8. monitor the results.

Overcome barriers

The first step in solving a problem is often to recognise that one exists, and while this may appear obvious it is often overlooked. To overcome barriers the leader needs to:

- *Ensure that problems are recognised* – team members need to understand clearly what should be given priority and what is important. Twenty years ago a customer complaint was not necessarily given much priority; today, in an age of service excellence, customer complaints are seen as problems themselves – and possibly symptoms of other problems as well!
- *Create an environment where problems are openly acknowledged.* Having recognised problems people need to be able to discuss how to resolve them and how to prevent them arising again. For this the culture needs to be positive, constructive and free of blame. Encouraging honesty and keeping an open-door policy also helps.
- *Create an environment that prevents and pre-empts difficulties before they arise.* This involves identifying areas of weakness or vital importance, and then monitoring them to ensure that any problems are prevented or resolved quickly. Considering possible solutions in advance can also prove useful (often known as scenario planning).

Define the problem

Ask the questions what, when, where and who? Remember what you are trying to achieve – go back to first principles – and see how much difficulty the problem is causing. Sometimes unplanned and even unwelcome events occur, but they may not necessarily be *problems*. If they do not cause ongoing difficulties or if there is simply nothing that can be done about them then it might, in certain instances, be better just to press on without attempting any 'corrective' action.

Gather relevant information

Don't be put off by distractions and ask:

- What is the problem? What is not the problem? What is affected by the problem?
- Who is affected? Who is not affected? What is different about those affected?
- What things are affected by the problem? What things are not affected? What is distinctive about those affected?

Identify possible causes

These may relate to people, systems or equipment. They may be external to the organisation or internal. Understanding the causes will help to highlight *where* action needs to be taken and *what* that action should be. It will also help to prevent the problem arising in the future.

Identify a possible solution

Remember that you are not only treating the symptoms, you need to get to the root of the problem and tackle the causes of the problem. They are also likely to impact on other areas, and it is certainly worth considering how the solution to one problem affects other parts of the task and the organisation. Techniques for finding the best solution include:

- *Brainstorming* – gathering as many ideas together as possible that might solve the problem – or form a part of the solution – and then assess each idea, seeing how practical it is, where it links with other ideas and whether it could provide the answer. The advantage of this approach is that it can often be free-flowing and imaginative, comprehensive and provide a range of options that can be prioritised and provide fall-back positions.
- *Discussing with others* – other views are also helpful in providing different perspectives. Generally, it helps to discuss the situation with people close to the action, as they have an understanding of what is feasible. However, if it is a complex problem it can help to strip it down to the bare facts and ask others who are not closely involved. This often helps to overcome the 'can't see the wood for the trees' syndrome, where the people dealing with the problem are too involved to evaluate potential solutions.
- *Research and analyse* – soliciting other opinions can be valuable in identifying problems and their solutions. For example, questionnaires and telephone research may help to provide guidance about what solutions would work, as well as other useful information such as how they should be implemented.

Check the solution

Imagine how the solution will work in practice, where it might fail, and adjust it if necessary.

- *Remember first principles* – with significant or complex problems it often helps to focus on the fundamental objectives: What are we trying to do? What action will bring the desired objective nearer?
- *Assess the likely consequences of the solution.* Solutions do not only need to solve the problem: they need to be workable and ensure that they do not simply create other difficulties.
- *Consider additional solutions and actions* – action may be needed in a number of areas and may need to be co-ordinated to ensure success.

Make the decision

Select the promising solution, plan its implementation and then stick with it! Common dangers at this point include:

- *Procrastinating and avoiding making a decision.* This will usually result in losing control.
- *Paralysis by analysis.* Over-analysing a situation can result in delay and ultimately has the same effect as procrastination.
- *Not managing risk.* The risk in any solution needs to be carefully assessed and it may be worth asking what is the *worst* that could happen; where are the weaknesses in this solution, and how can the risk be minimised. Is additional support required? Is a fall-back position required?
- *Disregarding intuition and experience.* The leader needs to be able to trust their own judgement and at times be prepared to rely on nothing more than intuition and experience. At moments like these it is worth remembering the old adage that the only certainties in life are death and taxes! In other words, most situations can be recovered.
- *Lacking confidence or conviction.* Confidence in the solution can be invaluable in implementing it and achieving success. A half-hearted approach is risky at best.

Monitor the results

Monitoring the effects of the solution enables any adjustments to be made. Even if the solution is not the best one it may still lead to the desired result with careful monitoring and some remedial action.

Summary: *Pitfalls in problem-solving*

Leaders can find that decisions and solutions are less effective – or even counter-productive – due to a range of factors. Behaviours to avoid in problem-solving include:

1. *Failing to define and understand the problem* – this can include failing to distinguish between causes and effects.
2. *Subjective, irrational analysis,* including prejudice or being unduly influenced by the 'halo' effect, when what is required is objective, unbiased analysis.
3. *Lack of rigorous, critical analysis* – casual complacency, arrogance, laziness, tiredness or overwork can all result in a lack of proper

analysis and a solution that fails to satisfactorily solve the problem.
4. *Laziness* – it is a mistake to avoid difficult or unpleasant solutions. Frequently the only way to achieve success is to earn it, and that requires commitment, hard work and leadership by example.
5. *Lack of sensitivity* – it is important to be able to anticipate problems and also to anticipate the full effects that their solutions will bring.
6. *Lack of focus and direction* – the leader needs to ensure that problem-solving is not hampered by a lack of clear objectives or priorities.
7. *Lack of creativity and innovation* – relying on experience or past approaches, even when tried and tested, may no longer be effective. Certain problems may require a devastatingly powerful new force in order for them to be resolved!
8. *Focus on peripheral issues, rather than substance* – sometimes the facts surrounding a problem are distracting or demanding in their own right, with the result that the problem is tinkered with or simply left to grow.
9. *Act appropriately, and where possible avoid quick and hasty action* – under the guise of being decisive it is often tempting to act without properly considering the best solution. This is further complicated by the fact that some situations actually require quick decisions. Knowing which approach fits each situation is therefore important for success.
10. *Over-confidence* – sometimes the solution may seem obvious, when in fact a better solution lies hidden elsewhere. It is wrong at *any* time to assume that they always have the best solution to any problem at their fingertips. Because of the constant pace of change the best solutions often need to be uncovered.
11. *Being too risk-averse* – part of successful leadership is the willingness and ability to take calculated risks. Hesitation and fear of failure may be natural but the leader needs to show the way in controlling risk and managing the situation.

Further information

Key Management Solutions
Tom Lambert, FT/Pitman, 1996

Practical Problem-Solving and Decision-Making
G. Wilson, Kogan Page, 1993

Practical Problem-Solving for Managers
M. Stephens, Kogan Page, 1988

Management Ideas in Brief
S. Kermally, Butterworth-Heinemann, 1996

Project management

Introduction

Project management is an aspect of leadership that is not defined by *what* one does, but rather by the *way* that it is done. It requires a set of highly developed skills and qualities in addition to leadership, including:

- planning skills
- problem-solving and lateral thinking abilities
- decision-making skills
- an understanding of the priorities, needs and concerns of the team
- sensitivity to the situation and the culture of the working environment
- the ability and confidence to know when to take a calculated risk
- a considerable level of personal commitment.

Project management is often mistakenly confused with operational management. When managing operations the focus is to achieve stability and consistency; the role of continuous improvement is vital, but essentially it is about managing a permanent, ongoing situation. With project management the aim is quite different: it is to achieve a limited set of objectives within an agreed amount of time, money and other resources.

The phases of a project are:

- *Start-up* – this might include bidding for a contract, assessing whether it is feasible and deciding what the objectives are to be.
- *Planning and preparation* – a vital aspect of managing and controlling a project is preparing thoroughly in advance.
- *Implementation* – the central part of the project, this involves executing the plan and delivering the final project.
- *Conclusion* – the point at which the project is completed. It is also useful for the leader to have a review session where the project team provides comments on how the project progressed, as this helps with improvements for the future.

Project management and leadership

Leading a project requires the ability to adopt the appropriate leadership style for each situation. The most frequently used leadership styles include acting as facilitator, arbitrator, coach, spokesperson, innovator, motivator, director (even at times an autocrat) and pacesetter. Project leadership requires, at various times:

- *Planning skills* – these need to be exercised across a range of different levels, from broad strategic plans to detailed operational plans.
- *Control skills* – the project leader needs to be sure that the project is proceeding as planned and needs to track:
    - expenditure against budget;
    - quality of work against agreed specifications;
    - progress against schedule.
- *Teamwork* – motivating, supporting and providing resources for your team;
- *Handling conflict and influencing people* – resolving differences between team members;
- *Decisiveness* and the ability to impose decisions, even when they are unpopular;
- *Communication skills* – so that the leader can inform and mobilise a range of different audiences that may be affected by the project, and maintain momentum and support.

Key techniques and concepts for managing projects

There are a large number of concepts and skills that are important in planning and managing successful projects. These include:

Dependencies

A dependency is an activity that is linked to other activities. In any project there will be some activities that need to happen sequentially, after others. Dependencies may be:

- *Internal* – these are activities under the project manager's control. An example would be mailing a marketing brochure that cannot happen until the brochure has been printed.
- *External* – these dependencies rely on something outside the project happening first; for instance, if the bank grants a loan then the business can expand.
- *Mandatory* – these are dependencies that are unavoidable and often involve physical constraints. For example, such as putting the roof on

PROJECT MANAGEMENT

the house after the walls have been built, or testing a new software program after it has been developed.
- *Discretionary* – these dependencies are decided by the project manager. For example, a house-builder may decide to make a selling point of the fact that buyers can choose their own fitted kitchens, and this means that the fitting has to wait until the houses are sold. It is often advisable to document discretionary dependencies.

Within these categories there are four further types of dependency:

1. *Finish-to-start* – this is the most common type of dependency where one activity starts only after another has finished. The activity may start immediately or there may be a time lag.
2. *Start-to-finish* – where one activity cannot finish before another has started, or where there is a known time relationship between one activity finishing and another starting.
3. *Finish-to-finish* – where activities must finish at the same time, or where there is a known relationship between the finish of two activities.
4. *Start-to-start* – where activities must start at the same time, or where there is a known relationship between the start of two activities.

Understanding where dependencies exist is a vital part of planning a project, as they impact on the timing and costs of projects. To identify dependencies it is often best to work backwards from the end result, as this will show what needs to be done in order to get there!

Flowcharts

A flowchart is a diagram clearly illustrating a sequence of interdependent activities. When managing operations, flowcharts are used to examine processes and look for ways that they may be improved. When managing projects they provide a map of all the activities that need to be done. A flowchart uses arrows and boxes to show the chronological flow of activities. The shape of each box is also significant and there are a large number of shapes used to represent different parts of the process. The most common basic shapes are:

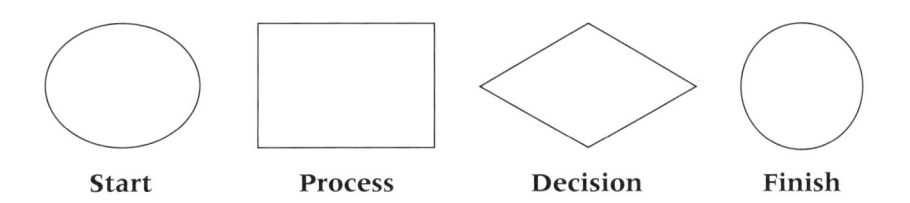

| Start | Process | Decision | Finish |

Flowcharts are useful for:

- Seeing the chronological flow of a project.
- Considering whether activities are happening in the most logical, effective way.
- Highlighting dependencies that may have been hidden – and understanding the *type* of dependency.
- Conceptualising projects. This is often useful for highlighting areas of weakness or lack of knowledge.

Work breakdown structure (WBS)

Flowcharts are inadequate for detailed scheduling and resource planning: what is required is a *work breakdown structure* that breaks a project down into separate elements that can be scheduled and costed. The process for developing a WBS is:

1. *Identify the main stages of the project* – these often correspond to the phases in the project's life cycle: initiation, design, construction, operation, evaluation.
2. *Divide each stage into smaller elements* – this can be done in a number of ways: some project managers group together stages which relate to each other, whereas others prefer to group together all those stages that relate to a specific *deliverable*. This latter approach is often preferable as it focuses on outcomes and is results-driven.
3. *Subdivide each stage into separate activities* – exactly how much subdivision into stages and tasks that is needed depends on the complexity of the project: the more complex it is then the more tiers there will be (often in more ways than one!). Activities need to be:
   - measurable in terms of cost, effort, resources and time required;
   - specific, in that they result in a clear outcome that can be acknowledged;
   - assigned to one individual who takes overall responsibility for completing the task.

Gantt charts

These are a highly effective method of representing a project plan so that it can be monitored, implemented and communicated. In essence it is a chart with time measured along the horizontal axis and activities listed vertically. Gantt charts can show activities that take place sequentially or in parallel, and can also highlight the critical path.

Simple Gantt chart

	Week 1	Week 2	Week 3	Week 4	Week 5	Week 6	Week 7
Task 1	▓▓▓▓	▓▓▓▓	▓▓▓▓				
Task 2		▓▓▓▓	▓▓▓▓				
Task 3				▓▓▓▓			
Task 4					▓▓▓▓	▓▓▓▓	
Task 5					▓▓▓▓		
Task 6						▓▓▓▓	▓▓▓▓

▬▬▬ denotes the critical path

Gantt charts have other benefits:

- they highlight where there is slack (or float) in the schedule;
- they can highlight relationships between activities;
- if generated on a software program they can be updated, enabling complex projects to be constantly monitored and implemented.

This last point highlights the value of project planning software, and it is particularly useful when planning the development of complex or detailed projects.

Schedules

The schedule lists the dates on which activities start and finish and they are usually shown as planned and actual. The time taken from the date the activity started to the date it was completed is known as the *lapsed time*, and the number of days within that period is the number of *man days*. So, for example, from the start of writing a book to the day it is completed may take three months (or ninety days) – this is the lapsed time. However, writing will not take place all day everyday, but may only require one month – or thirty man days – within that period.

Milestones

Milestones are important dates within the project schedule and usually occur either at the end of a task or the completion of a deliverable. Milestones can be useful tools for several reasons:

- they are useful moments to pause and review progress: assess how things have happened and what needs to alter in the future;

- they are psychological points that maintain momentum for the project, and can be used to motivate people and celebrate success;
- they are useful practical points at which suppliers can be paid, new resources can be brought in and existing ones finished.

Budgets

Setting and controlling budgets is an important aspect of project management. Project budgets normally include:

- *Material costs* – these are the supplies that are used during the project and are usually highest during the project's *implementation* phase. They tend to be directly attributable to specific tasks and are therefore classed as direct costs.
- *Labour costs* – these include all payments made to people involved in the project: consultants as well as staff, and like material costs they tend to be highest during the implementation phase. They can either be *direct* costs, associated with a specific task or group of tasks; or *indirect* costs that support the programme overall.
- *Equipment costs* – these can include hiring tools or facilities for the duration of the project. Again they are either direct or indirect costs.
- *Additional costs* – there will probably be other costs that arise, depending on the nature of the project. For example a publishing project may involve copyright fees and royalties; a building project may involve the costs of obtaining planning permission.
- *Contingency* – much of the ultimate success and credibility of the project rests on achieving it within agreed costs. Costs can easily escalate over time, and if the project is not carefully planned then some costs will be overlooked. Even if projects are meticulously planned, and even if the price for work in the project remains unchanged, they can still absorb more money than planned to:
  - cope with unforeseen circumstances
  - exploit unforeseen opportunities
  - allow for mistakes that are made.

A contingency is therefore an essential part of the budget and needs to provide a realistic safety net.

Project plans

The most practical and effective way to manage a project is to start by developing a project plan that will guide you through the implementation phase of the project. The plan will have many features depending on the type of project and the needs of the project leader, however it would normally include the following features:

Terms of reference or contract

This should include:

- a statement of the project objectives
- details of the deliverables for the project
- details relating to timing, specifications and costs
- information about reporting arrangements for the project
- procedures to follow, should problems arise.

Work breakdown structure

This is normally detailed enough to ensure satisfactory control of the project's implementation phase: it can include:

- sufficiently detailed specifications for each task
- a Gantt chart and project schedule (including start and finish dates and major milestones).

Budget/project costing

The plan should include estimates, ideally binding, for all work required in the WBS.

Project team

This section needs to include details of personnel involved in the project: their roles and responsibilities, possibly including job descriptions. It should also be communicated to – and understood by – everyone involved.

Management plan

This includes:

- Procedures for dealing with specific issues such as handling the media, dealing with crises, gaining approval for expenditure.
- The areas of greatest risk in the project clearly highlighted, together with planned measures to reduce risk or handle situations should they arise.
- Any other issues that may be ongoing or unresolved where the project leader will need to make decisions.
- Additional documentation that may be referred to during the implementation phase.

Successfully planning a project requires:

- a knowledge of project management techniques;
- some understanding and expertise in the area of the project;
- the ability to take an overview of the whole project, combined with an attention to detail, ensuring that each aspect is successfully implemented;
- the ability to manage organisational structures, processes and culture so as *to make things happen*;
- leadership skills and the ability to get the best from people.

> **Summary:** *Key issues for project leaders*
>
> There are a number of key questions that project leaders should consider at each stage of the process:
>
> **Start-up phase**
>
> - Is this project feasible?
> - Will it be profitable?
> - How will it relate to other areas of work – will it help or hinder?
> - What are the benefits and disadvantages of undertaking this project?
> - Is the necessary time available to devote to it?
> - What will happen if it is not undertaken?
> - What will happen if it goes wrong?
>
> **Planning phase**
>
> - What are the biggest obstacles to this project?
> - What resources will be needed?
> - Are the required resources available? If not, where can they be found?
> - Do we have the right people in the right jobs?
> - Do the members of the project team clearly understand their roles?
> - Are team members adequately trained and prepared?
> - Have the costs been planned?
> - What contingencies are there in the project, especially for cost and time overruns?
> - Has the risk in the project been assessed?
> - Are the project dependencies understood?
> - Where and when are the critical points in the project?

- Do people understand the processes and procedures that need to be followed?
- Is the project implementation planned as efficiently as possible?

Implementation phase

- Is the project proceeding at the right pace, with momentum, according to plan?
- Is the team working well?
- Are there any long-term difficulties that need to be addressed?
- What are the short-term problems and how are these being resolved?
- Is everybody working to full capacity?
- Are there regular reviews to monitor progress?

Conclusion

- Could the project have been less expensive?
- Could it have been completed quicker?
- Were there the right people in the project team? If not, what skills were absent and what areas could have been better?
- What were the main areas of weakness?
- Did communications work well during the project?
- What aspect of the project's management would you do differently in the future?

Further information

Managing Successful Projects
P. Baguley, FT/Pitman, 1995

The Project Workout
R. Buttrick, FT/Pitman, 1997

A Practical Guide to Project Planning
C. Burton and N. Michael, Kogan Page, 1994

Staff planning and interviewing

Introduction

The leader's role in planning for new staff has three key elements:

1. *Staff planning* – deciding what jobs need new or additional people
2. *Job descriptions and person specifications* – deciding what skills those new people need for those jobs
3. *Interviewing and recruiting* – finding and selecting the right people.

Often a personnel department helps the leader in these tasks, but it is important to remember that ultimately it is the leader who is responsible for the work that is done.

Staff planning

Approaches to staff planning can vary considerably depending on the size of the organisation, and staff planning itself is a subset of the broader strategic planning process. The basic process involves:

1. Forecasting sales and planning future production or service levels.
2. Estimating the amount and type of work that will be required.
3. Deciding what skills are required, who will do this work, what training and development needs exist and what the recruitment needs are to fill the gaps.
4. Implementing the plan – recruiting, transferring and training people – monitoring the process and evaluating its success.

Forecasting

This needs to be done for a wide variety of reasons – from managing suppliers to planning cash flow – and it underpins the staff planning process.

Estimating future work requirements

Timing is critical to the staff planning process: appoint people too early and they will be an expensive, underutilised drain on resources; appoint too late and they will still be training and finding the ropes when they should be hitting their stride. To avoid this:

- *Analyse current and future jobs* – understand what is involved, avoiding assumptions, and ideally discuss with other people that may already be doing the job. How long does it take to train? What changes and pressures will be faced? What skills are vital and what are desirable?
- *Decide what to do about fluctuations in workload* – if workloads are likely to vary, for example, because of a major project or for seasonal reasons, then this should be taken into account. It might mean, for example, that part-time or temporary (fixed-term) contracts are needed.

Profiling the workforce and deciding what skills are required

Profiling the work force means asking questions such as:

- What is the level of staff turnover?
- What are the reasons for staff turnover?
- What is the current level of productivity? (An easy method for monitoring this is dividing revenue by the number of staff.)
- How much money is available for recruitment (both to find and train the right person and then to employ them)?
- What are the likely consequences of recruitment? These might mean that supervisors have to take on greater responsibility; is this feasible? Will *they* need to be paid more?

The outcome of profiling should be a clear picture of the management action needed and a clear understanding of the skills required. There may be staff already in place who can be appointed to fill the new jobs. The final phase is to recruit people and this has two key elements: developing a person specification and interviewing.

Job descriptions and person specifications

Job descriptions

After assessing the tasks involved, the next stage is to prepare an outline of what the job-holder must do. The description should be brief and serve as a useful reference for the manager and the individual. It can include:

- job title
- line manager
- subordinates
- key relationships with other departments, job holders, customers and suppliers
- the purpose of the job (a brief overview of the job)
- overall responsibilities and tasks (a list of what the job-holder needs to do)

- working hours
- special needs (e.g. areas where the job-holder needs to refer to their line manager).

Job descriptions should be kept current and can be reviewed following an appraisal, bearing in mind that both the job and the person's skills will develop. (Research indicates that the average length of time for one person to do the same job is 10 months, so it would seem sensible to assume that the job description should be reviewed, on average, every 10 months too.)

Person specification

This is based on the task analysis and details the skills, knowledge and experience that are required. It is useful for preparing job advertisements, assessing internal applicants and interviewing external ones. It is important that the specification is *realistic*. It is also useful to set out the *minimum* qualities that a candidate must possess, and then to add other *desirable* elements. The areas to consider including are:

- skills and abilities
- experience
- personal qualities (such as their level of motivation, flexibility or initiative)
- technical expertise
- qualifications needed
- special circumstances (e.g. non-smoker, car driver).

Interviewing

Interviewing: the WASP process

A common process for interviews is WASP: Welcome, Acquire Information, Supply Information, Part. (Some people prefer to provide information about the job *before* asking questions; however, the danger here is that the candidate will then simply tailor their answers to what the interviewer has said they want!)

1. *Welcome* – putting the candidate at their ease is a useful first step and this can be done by small talk, quickly leading in to a short overview of what the job is followed by the interviewer's questions.
2. *Acquire information* – still keeping the candidate at their ease, the interview should then move on to questions. Why did you decide to apply for the job? Describe your career to date? are useful introductions to this part of the process as they are often expected and focus on the individual. Starting with broader questions: like these will enable the

interviewer to find areas to explore in further detail that should highlight the candidate's suitability.
3. *Supply information* – explain further about:

- the organisation: its key features, aims and objectives.
- the tasks involved in the job.
- reporting arrangements, including the name and title of their line manager; key relationships within the organisation and, for a supervisory role, who will be reporting to the candidate.
- terms and conditions of employment.

4. *Part* – this should include:

- Asking the candidate if they have any questions: good candidates probably will, and these need to be answered fully.
- Explaining the selection process and what happens next.
- Thanking the candidate for their time.

Useful tips when interviewing

- Control the interview. Prepare your questions; find out about the candidate beforehand; focus yourself and the candidate on important issues; avoid talking too much yourself or focusing on minor points or irrelevancies, and manage your use of time.
- Ask specific but open questions which allow the candidate to freely express themselves.
- Never mislead the candidate, for example, by omitting details of mundane or difficult tasks. This will only cause problems, difficulties and possibly expense later.
- Rephrase questions that you believe that the candidate has not satisfactorily answered (simply repeating may seem rude and bullying).
- Do not ask questions too rapidly.
- Be polite and stay interested.
- Do not rush to fill silences or put words in the candidate's mouth.
- Don't offer the candidate the job during the interview unless you are *absolutely certain*.
- Make notes and evaluate the interview immediately afterwards.

Appointing staff

Finally, useful tips to remember when appointing people are:

- *Check references.* This does not necessarily need to be done by post, often a phone call will suffice. The advantages of phone calls are that you can, with the obvious agreement of the individual, discuss the person's

strengths and weaknesses; even if you have decided to go ahead with the appointment you will at least have a more balanced view of the individual.
- *Confirm details (including start date, pay and benefits) in writing* to prevent any misunderstanding and to act as an aide-memoire (for both sides) in the future.
- *Ensure compliance with relevant employment law legislation.* All developed countries currently have a raft of employment law legislation, and the trend is for this to continue increasing. A vital role for the personnel function is to advise on complying with the law: ignorance is no defence. In particular, consider the legal implications of:
    - staff recruitment and discrimination legislation
    - employing foreign nationals and immigration law
    - trade unions and transfer of undertakings
    - European employment legislation which affects such issues as maternity and paternity rights, working hours and other important conditions of employment.
- *Consider what is best practice when appointing people and how it looks.* Taking on a member of staff can send a message to people inside and outside the organisation, and it is worth remembering that your organisation may well be affected by the manner in which you appoint people. For example, an organisation that continually hires and fires will soon get a reputation for this and may find it harder to attract the right people. Humorous job advertisements may be designed to attract a certain group, but how will they appear to customers? Similarly, advertisements that are ageist have declined considerably in recent years and are certainly not best practice.
- *Check that everyone (and everything) is ready.* There is nothing worse than making someone feel that their first day (or week) is an afterthought: it makes the job of motivation and management much harder.
    - inform people who is starting, when and what their job (and job title) is
    - consider organising an induction programme that is relevant for the new recruit
    - ensure that there are the necessary resources available when the person starts.
- *Use probation periods.* A probation period, normally three months, is useful when making certain staff appointments. In essence, the person knows that they are not confirmed in the job until their probation period has passed satisfactorily. This protects both the employee and employer and provides an opportunity to review progress early on.

- *Consider what notice period is appropriate.* Many organisations have one standard notice period for everyone, regardless of the job they do and the time it would take to appoint and train a replacement, and this is often the result of inertia or simply not understanding the job role and people involved. The leader should ensure that notice periods are correct and appropriate.
- *Set direction, starting as you mean to go on.* How each individual is managed depends on each leadership style. However, the best approach is usually:
    - To grant some latitude at the start of the appointment – enabling the new recruit to fully understand the team and task requirements as well as the culture of the organisation.
    - To manage people consistently from the start so that they are clear about what is expected of them.
    - To make the best use of the person from the outset; often leaders have had such a battle to find the right person that they relax too soon!
    - To provide direction, guidance and support, and monitor the new person's progress.

Summary: *Preventing potential problems*

These points are important as they act as a failsafe to ensure that the appointment is right, preventing problems later, as well as protecting both the employer and employee. Finally, it is increasingly common for rejected candidates to contact interviewers and ask specifically why they were rejected, and whether they could do anything to improve their chances with another employer. This takes courage but can provide valuable results for the candidate, and the interviewer should be prepared to justify their decision if asked to do so.

Further information

One Stop Personnel
D. Martin, ICSA Publishing, second edition 1999

Handbook of Management
D. Lock (Editor), Gower, 1995

Finding and Keeping the Right People
J. Billsberry, FT/Pitman, 1996

Handbook of Personnel Management Practice
M. Armstrong, Kogan Page, 1996

Recruiting: How to do it
Iain Maitland, Cassell, 1997

Strategic planning

Introduction

In a constantly changing and shifting work environment a strategy for achieving the organisation's purpose is invaluable; this is particularly the case for commercial businesses facing competitive pressures. A strategic plan is a map for reaching the organisation's goals, and it is often subdivided into a business plan that includes at least a budget and marketing plan for each operating unit, leading to objectives for each department, team and ultimately each individual. (In small businesses the strategic plan and business plan are often the same.) This section examines techniques for developing an effective strategy.

Developing a strategy

A strategy goes right to the core of the organisation, guiding its future. It needs to be based on several central questions:

- What business are we in?
- What is our purpose?
- Where are we now?
- Where do we want to be in the future?
- How will we achieve this?

Benefits of strategic planning

Strategic plans provide:

- a sense of purpose, energy and direction;
- a means of communicating, motivating and co-ordinating efforts across the organisation;
- a focus on key areas for development and activity, and issues such as productivity, quality and profitability;
- an opportunity to change the nature of the organisation – its purpose, activities and even its culture;
- a set of guiding principles as well as a practical framework for producing objectives that can be cascaded throughout the organisation to each individual;

- a means of informing and improving strategic decisions;
- a means of measuring performance;
- a way of consulting staff, generating new insights and ideas and gaining employees' commitment.

Key aspects of strategic plans

Strategic plans need to be:

- *Flexible and endure* – taking account of changing circumstances without being rewritten.
- *Realistic* – plans must take account of external and internal realities. They need to be visionary but practical; challenging but feasible; practical but not mundane.
- *Innovative* – the reason the organisation needs a plan is to make it the best at what it does, this is likely to require a creative, distinctive approach.
- *Focused* – clear, understandable and able to generate commitment at any level in the organisation.
- *Up-to-date* – obsolete plans are a sign of an organisation that is, at best, at drift – and probably in decline. It is vital that the organisation clearly knows where it is going and how it will get there. If this means that the planned direction needs to alter from time to time then this should be reflected in the plan.

Techniques for strategic planning

1. *Consult as widely as possible* – organisations often restrict strategic planning to senior managers with the result that plans are unrealistic and alien to the people who are expected to implement them. Involving a wide range of people – including shareholders (and other stakeholders in not-for-profit organisations) as well as employees – gains valuable ideas, perspectives and contributions.
2. *Analyse the organisation's present position and current trends* – the position needs to be assessed relative to both its competitors, and where it wants to be. Asking several key questions (perhaps in the form of a questionnaire) will help to define what the strategy should be:

    - What is the organisation's current position? (This leads to other questions, for example, large commercial businesses will need to know what is happening to market share.)
    - How did it get there – what factors were important?
    - What are the main strengths and weaknesses of the organisation in relation to the competition?
    - What are the main external opportunities and threats?

- How is the organisation perceived? (Questioning the corporate identity will help to provide a clear picture of *all* aspects of the organisation, and leads to other illuminating questions such as how is morale? What kind of leadership is exerted, and what are the organisation's *values*?)
- Is the trend for greater success or less?
- How is morale at present?

In looking for answers to these questions the leader needs to find evidence, rather than basing their findings on what they believe to be the case. This means understanding the reality of the present situation and gaining a balanced view of the *whole* organisation – its strengths *and* its weaknesses.

3. *Decide what business you are in* – focus on the purpose of the organisation: why it exists and what it is there to do. This may mean departing from the obvious or questioning fundamentals. For example, one world famous maker of fountain pens sees itself in the gift business, competing with manufacturers of cigarette lighters. A publishing company sees itself in the information business competing with electronic networks and television. When deciding what business you are in you should:

- Carefully consider where the organisation is at present.
- Take a broad but balanced view of the opportunities (i.e. be as broad as possible without losing focus, synergy and appeal). Too narrow a perspective can miss opportunities; too broad and there are risks and learning curves of diversification.
- Decide whether you want to expand into new areas or keep with core activities.

4. *Decide where the organisation is going and set a clear direction* – this involves setting a clear, powerful *vision* for the future with objectives for how to get there. An effective vision needs to be a clear statement of *what* business the organisation is in; *where* it is going and *how* it will get there. Vision or mission statements need to:

- Be in touch with reality.
- Be clearly understood by everyone in the organisation.
- Send a clear message inside and outside the organisation to stakeholders and the market.
- Be inspirational and challenging but realistic.
- Motivate people and gain their commitment.

5. *Establish time frames* – visions are usually longer-term, perhaps taking as long as ten years to achieve, as organisations (particularly in business) need time to change attitudes and build or shift resources. (However,

the trend is for organisations to have shorter and shorter horizons for their visions.)

The strategic planning process needs to provide objectives and targets that are attainable within a much shorter time frame – usually 3–5 years. This is necessary in order to motivate people around a practical time frame, keep a clear focus on what needs to be done (without guessing too much about the future), and to generate momentum.

6. *Set clear objectives and implement the strategic plan* – the leaders of the organisation need to translate the vision into practical objectives – a strategic plan – that can be acted upon by the whole organisation. The strategic plan needs to:

    - Take into account the organisation's *internal* areas of weakness and provide a framework for improving them.
    - Consider likely future *external* developments that will affect the organisation and outline how they will be handled (i.e. with increased investment, diversification, consolidation).
    - Be translated into objectives that are measurable, attainable and time-constrained. This can be achieved by focusing on each area of the organisation. For a business this means:
        - financial issues of profitability and return on investment (ROI);
        - marketing issues of market share, brand-building and meeting market needs;
        - leadership issues of participation, innovation and commitment;
        - corporate issues of growth and public responsibility.
    - Be widely communicated and understood so that people can give their full commitment.

7. *Evaluate and adapt the strategic plan* – the purpose of the strategic plan is to produce results that realise the vision of the organisation: this is not feasible if the plan keeps changing significantly and if the direction of the organisation varies. However, the one constant is to stay close to the market, and this means continuous improvement and development for the organisation, and continuous measurement of progress against the plan. To account for this process of constant change it is wise to evaluate and modify the plan on a rolling basis: reviewing and adapting five year plans every three years, and three year plans every two. This also ensures that:

    - The plan is kept relevant and realistic.
    - Changing circumstances are accounted for and new opportunities or problems are faced.

- The commitment of employees is refreshed and reinvigorated.

> **Summary:** *The strategic planning process*
>
> There are a number of practical tips to consider when undertaking a strategic planning process:
>
> - Keep the process of strategic planning as simple as possible, and schedule it.
> - Consult as widely as possible – not only within the organisation but with others (e.g. the organisation's shareholders, accountants, advisers). Organisations often use external advisers – or simply get away from the business for a few days – in order to ensure a fresh perspective.
> - The process of strategic review is essentially consultative: ultimately it is the leaders that need to decide what course to take.
> - In gaining people's commitment it often helps to explain why decisions have been reached, and why certain possibilities have been discarded.
> - Leaders should regularly (i.e. every month or so) remind themselves of their strategic plan – what they are aiming to achieve.
>
> The process of strategic planning itself shows an organisation and leadership that is getting to grips with its own destiny: it is a vitally important aspect of leadership, potentially rewarding and significant.

Further information

Exploring Corporate Strategy
G. Johnson and K. Scholes, Prentice Hall, 1999

Competing for the Future
G. Hamel and C.K. Prahalad, Harvard University Press, 1994

The Rise and Fall of Strategic Planning
H. Mintzberg, Prentice Hall, 1994

Competitive Advantage – Creating and sustaining superior performance
M. Porter, The Free Press, 1985

Strategic Control
M. Goold, J. Quinn, Ashridge, 1990

In Search of Excellence
T. Peters and R. Waterman, Harper and Row, 1982

Stress management

Introduction

The issue of stress is one that has finally become acknowledged and accepted in the workplace, and with this has come a recognition of the sources of stress, the scope of the problem and a range of strategies to reduce and handle stress. Whilst some controlled measure of stress is actually useful – ensuring that concentration is heightened and performance improved accordingly – the consequences of stress are particularly important for leaders in three ways:

1. It reduces the leader's own personal effectiveness.
2. It can reduce staff morale and sap the team's ability to achieve the desired goals.
3. It can reduce the overall efficiency and damage the external perception of the whole organisation.

For these reasons leaders need to be able to manage their own stress; create conditions that reduce the level and incidence of stress in their organisation, and detect the symptoms of stress in others.

Understanding and preventing stress

Recognising stress at work in yourself and others

It is often difficult to know when one is suffering from stress – or the danger of it – because it builds up gradually over time and is all-consuming, being difficult to separate from normal behaviour. Stress is a personal matter, and the symptoms are behavioural, or physical, or both. Physical symptoms of stress include a wide range of changes such as:

- irregular breathing
- feeling tense and stiff
- stomach complaints (such as indigestion or ulcers)
- exhaustion and tiredness
- tension headaches
- twitching
- fidgeting and feeling restless or 'on edge'
- a dry mouth and throat

- feeling hot
- clammy hands and perspiration
- sexual problems.

All of these problems can occur at different times for many reasons quite unrelated to stress, however, they may well be stress-related if several occur at the same time, if they appear constantly, or if they appear without apparent cause.

The behavioural symptoms of stress are no less significant or serious, and include:

- feeling worried
- demotivated
- irritated
- withdrawn
- upset
- exhausted or weary
- angry, misunderstood
- frustrated and
- powerless.

These in turn lead to difficulties in concentrating, focusing, being creative, making decisions or solving problems – in short, judgement is impaired and the stressed individual is not working normally. Loss of appetite or weight gain, smoking, alcoholism and even drug abuse may all be symptoms of stress.

Individual reactions to stress vary, and it is also worth pointing out that different people seem to have different levels at which they suffer from stress, based on their personality and life experiences. In assessing your own level of stress you should understand your personal stress threshold. If you are unsure, the best approach is to ask yourself if this situation would normally upset you. If you suspect you might be stressed, or especially if someone else mentions it to you, it may be worth questioning your own pattern of behaviour: Are you behaving as you would normally do (or react)? Would you have behaved like this last year? Is there something significant that is constantly on your mind?

However, one of the most common reactions to stress is the amplification of personality traits: for example, irritable people may become explosive, or quiet people become completely withdrawn. To recognise stress, therefore, it is important to distinguish typical patterns of behaviour from unusual ones. There is also a self-reinforcing 'downward cycle' of stress: many of the symptoms, such as anger or inefficiency, prevent the problem being solved, and more than that they actually *exacerbate* the situation and cause greater stress leading to more problems, and greater stress …

STRESS MANAGEMENT

Understanding the causes of stress

There are a number of careers – and aspects of careers – which are recognised as being highly stressful, but the truth is that anyone, at any level in any job, can suffer from stress at some time.

The causes and symptoms of stress at work can often be the same, and include a broad range of factors such as:

- work overload and an increase in out-of-hours working
- absenteeism due to ill health
- high employee turnover
- reduced job satisfaction
- break down in communication
- a focus on unproductive tasks.

and any number of other factors contributing to poor performance or a lack of success. In fact, the common causes of stress at work can be broken down into five key areas:

1. *Factors that are an integral part of the job* – these can typically include environmental issues (e.g. privacy, noise, comfort); time pressures; career development issues (e.g. pay and conditions); prolonged travel or learning new skills (e.g. technology).
2. *Factors that relate to the role and what the person actually does* – for leaders this cause of stress is perhaps the greatest, as leaders have responsibility for resources (people, equipment, money) and controlling these is highly dependent on unpredictable external forces, such as relationships, customers and the work environment. Also, the task of leadership is essentially about making choices and this usually brings its own conflict, to a greater or lesser degree, that can cause stress.
3. *Relationships* – for many complex reasons working relationships can be very difficult to manage, leading to stress. Good communications, respect and trust provide good foundations, but these are not (and cannot) always be present, and when they are absent the end result is often stress. Although one of the more serious causes of stress, relationships do also offer the most promise for improving the situation and ending the stress. It is often obvious when a relationship is causing stress, and there are often many ways to try and reduce its stressful effects.
4. *Organisational change* – generally people can be very wary of change, and when the change is significant and affects, possibly even threatens, a major part of someone's life, then the result is normally concern and stress. This might result from a change in responsibilities; relocation; redundancy, merger or acquisition.
5. *Life causes of stress* – stress at work may not originate at work, but could

187

be caused by events or issues from home. The most powerful are the death of someone close, divorce or separation from a partner, or moving house. Interestingly, other supposedly joyful times can also cause worry and stress, notably weddings, pregnancy and holidays!

Stress is highly complex and is rarely caused by one factor alone: it is not only the *range of issues* that cause stress, but the type of individual experiencing it *and how they react.*

Checklist – minimising and handling your own stress

- *Know yourself* – understand what causes *you* stress, when you are likely to become stressed and how you can avoid these situations.
- *Take responsibility* – too often people either deny their problem, in which case it will almost certainly worsen, or blame someone (or something) else. Even if it is the fault of someone else it is *you* that is being affected and *you* that needs to resolve it. People are often too afraid, ashamed or uncertain to admit that they are suffering from stress, but the longer they delay the worse become the effects of the downward cycle.
- *Consider what is causing stress* – is it resulting from the job, your role, work relationships, change, or something else, perhaps not work related at all? Knowing the symptoms and acknowledging the existence of stress is really only the start: the next key step is to identify the source of the stress. This is often complicated by the fact that stress may often be caused by an accumulation of factors piling up on each other. The solution is to consider rationally how to take down the wall that is encircling you, brick by brick. Stress is rarely removed in one go, but often requires action in a range of areas.
- *Anticipate stressful periods (either at work or home) and plan for them* – this may include getting temporary resources or people with specific skills to help during a particular period.
- *Develop strategies for handling stress* – consider what may have worked for you in the past, what you did and how successful it was. Also consider removing or reducing the cause of stress, or learning to accept it if it cannot be removed.
- *Understand and use management techniques to prevent or reduce stress* – for example, time management and assertiveness are two of the most important skills in reducing and handling stress, as many difficulties are caused either by time pressures or relationship issues that could be prevented by more assertive, controlled behaviour. Communication, decision-making and problem-solving also have much to offer once the problem has been acknowledged and the sources of stress are identified.
- *Relax* – easier said than done, but the key is to understand that you need to *work* at relaxing! This may mean planning a holiday or finding a

hobby or club that suits you best, and then *absorbing* yourself in it. Time away from the causes of stress can help to put the situation in perspective and lead to a new approach that provides a solution.

Preventing and reducing stress within organisations

As a leader it is possible to reduce stress for others by developing good communication systems, a supportive team approach, a blame-free environment, and a clear sense of involvement and responsibility. Other factors that can also help include mentoring schemes that prevent, identify and treat cases of stress; appraisal systems, and simply knowing and understanding the people that work with you. For some senior managers in large organisations this may not be possible, in which case these values need to be passed down the chain of command so that they are supported throughout the organisation.

Recent developments

At the time of writing the Health and Safety Executive (HSE) had suggested that there should be legislation which would directly combat stress at work. In a consultation document 'Managing Stress at Work' (reference DDE10, available from HSE Books) the HSE concentrates on three main themes:

1. the general effect of stress
2. whether it should be regulated under health and safety law
3. if so, if the existing Health and Safety at Work Act 1974 is necessarily the best vehicle or if there should be a specific or new Act.

The HSE has also issued a booklet seeking to provide guidance to employers on how they can act to reduce or prevent work-related stress by providing support and training, and setting reasonable targets. (Contact: HSE Books, PO Box 1999, Sudbury, Suffolk CO10 6FS. Tel: 01787 881165.)

The Loss Prevention Council (operated by the insurance industry) seeks to try to help to minimise claims. Recognising the potentially high costs of claims associated with workplace stress it has published 'Work Stress – advice on prevention and management' and 'Work Stress – a brief guide for line managers'. (Contact: Publications Dept, Loss Prevention Council, Melrose Avenue, Borehamwood, WD6 2BJ.)

> **Summary:** *Preventing and handling stress*
>
> To reduce and handle your own levels of stress you should start by understanding yourself, and consider what you would recognise as the symptoms of stress for you. To help, it can be useful to think about previous times that were stressful and remember how you felt, how you reacted and behaved, what the result was and whether, with the benefit of hindsight, you handled it in the best way possible.
>
> As a leader you should not be afraid to mention to someone if you think they are suffering from stress, and be prepared to help and support them in breaking the downward cycle. Often, just acknowledging the existence of stress and showing understanding can provide enough energy to see the solution, remove the stress and ultimately overcome the problem.

Further information

Successful Stress Management in a Week
A. Straw and C. Cooper, Hodder Headline, 1993

Coping with Stress
H. Greenberg, Prentice Hall, 1980

Managing Stress
D. Fontana, British Psychological Society, 1989

Pressure at Work
T. Arroba and K. James, McGraw-Hill, 1992

Team-building and developing high-performing teams

Introduction

Teams and team-based working has developed into the normal way of structuring organisations and undertaking tasks, yet it is a difficult and complex aspect of leadership and is usually developed through experience. Every leader has their own style, and when developing a high-performing team this needs to combine with an understanding of:

- *the benefits of team-building* – what it can achieve and what the leader should be striving for;
- *team roles and dynamics* – how teams work and achieve their greatest success;
- *the key stages of team development* – what they are and how to support the team in each stage;
- *the features of a successful team and team leader;*
- *how to avoid potential problems and pitfalls.*

Developing a high-performing team

The benefits of team-building

Team-building normally requires assiduous hard work, commitment and painful experience before success is achieved. It is therefore worth considering why team-building is important to leadership and what it delivers:

1. *Organisations become more effective and cohesive*

- employees are involved in the management and development of processes: their first-hand knowledge, experience and ability is used;
- people work together, passing on their knowledge and experience;
- individuals have greater ownership, responsibility and motivation;
- team members' involvement leads to realistic plans and objectives;
- team working fosters loyalty and a common determination to achieve success;

- teams break down departmental barriers, bringing people (and their ideas, skills and experiences) together;
- people feel more valued and are consequently more inclined to help and be supportive during difficulties;
- members conform their working habits to fit with the team, encouraging more disciplined working practices.

2. *Greater innovation often results from team working*

- teams that are working well provide an excellent environment for discussing problems, new ideas, opportunities and better ways of working;
- team working promotes creative thought and the free exchange of ideas;
- teams provide quicker implementation of new ideas and faster feedback, making the organisation more adaptable and capable.

3. *Individuals develop their skills and perform their job better*

- job satisfaction increases, people are more relaxed and hence more likely to do their job well;
- conflict is reduced and problems are solved quickly and effectively;
- team members take greater responsibility themselves – monitoring their own performance and providing feedback – and this advances the range of what the organisation can achieve;
- individual skills and abilities are fully used, rather than being underdeveloped or locked away.

Understanding team roles

Meredith Belbin has devised a hugely popular method of understanding the ways that people work together in teams. He identified eight types of preferred ways that people work in teams and some of the essential characteristics are highlighted in Table 6.

It should be emphasised that these team types are *preferred ways of working*, meaning that some people may exhibit characteristics from a number of categories but one style tends to dominate the way they work in a team. Understanding and managing these individual styles effectively is seen as being important in developing and leading effective teams.

Belbin's team preferences and their characteristics	Key points for leaders
1. THE IMPLEMENTOR • Diligent and action-oriented; self-motivated individuals that get things done • Good planners and well-organised administrators • Tend to be knowledgeable and respected in their specialist field	• Implementors help to focus the team on tasks • They focus on objectives – and often help to define them if necessary • They are calm and reliable under pressure, and are prepared to persevere • They provide practical support to others in the team Weaknesses include: 1. Insensitive to the suggestions of others 2. They can lack flexibility **Summary: implementors – also known as company workers – are vital members of the team: they are efficient, effective and practical.**
2. THE CO-ORDINATOR • Controls, organises and marshals the team – like the conductor in an orchestra • Tends to stand back from the team, providing comments from a different perspective • Is skilled at getting people to work together • Helps team members to understand their roles and what they need to do • Is encouraging, supportive and provides positive feedback • Co-ordinates resources well and delegates effectively • Identifies weaknesses in the team and takes action to develop the team	• Co-ordinators are well-placed to manage the team; they can stand back from the detail and mobilise people to tackle the right issues • They tend to be effective communicators with good interpersonal skills Weaknesses include: 1. Competitive with other team types, and will abdicate leadership in the face of strong competition (e.g. from Shapers). 2. Do not necessarily have a creative or challenging aspect to their role 3. Can be too aloof from the action to recognise the team's full capabilities

Belbin's team preferences and their characteristics	Key points for leaders
• Perseveres and acts as a focus for the team's efforts – particularly when under pressure	**Summary: commands respect, steady, patient, assured, but radical or creative thinking is not their strength.**

3. THE SHAPER

• Injects energy and momentum into the team's activities: takes action and makes things happen • Provides shape, direction and focus to the team, setting objectives and exerting a directive influence on team discussions • Summarises outcomes • Has a broad perspective of the team's goals and, like the Co-ordinator, helps team members to understand their roles and what they need to do • Challenges others views and can be demanding	• Shapers work most effectively in a team of peers • They are energetic and practical and this should be harnessed and channelled by the leader Weaknesses of Shapers that the leader should avoid: 1. Their directive 'broad brush' style that can ignore detail and undermine authority. 2. Insensitivity and lack of tact that can lead to competitiveness and even isolation. **Summary: dynamic, outgoing, energetic but can be tense.**

4. THE PLANT

• Creative, innovative people that constantly generate radical new ideas • Provide a new, independent perspective • Focus on big issues, formulating new approaches and looking for breakthroughs • Contributions are well-timed and appropriate	• Plants are a valuable resource offering ideas and creativity, and these need to be focused; often their ideas can range too broadly if not directed Weaknesses: 1. Can be self-indulgent, possibly ignoring the needs of the team when suggesting solutions. 2. Can be sensitive. This may result in being inhibited in their

TEAM-BUILDING AND DEVELOPING HIGH-PERFORMING TEAMS

Belbin's team preferences and their characteristics	Key points for leaders
	contributions (although they have good ideas to suggest), or not taking criticism of their ideas well
	Summary: serious, individualistic, highly intelligent and focused on the big issues, but can be impractical and focused on their own ideas.
5. THE RESOURCE INVESTIGATOR • A networker that develops the team's external resources • Works independently, quickly making contacts, developing and harnessing resources • Is interested in new ideas and explores outside possibilities • Has excellent interpersonal skills and maintains good team relationships, providing encouragement and support, especially under pressure	• Resource investigators are creative people with good communication skills and they bring a fresh perspective (along with contacts and resources) to the team Weaknesses include: 1. Can work too much in isolation: they focus on their own ideas and often reject ideas and information before raising them with the team. 2. Can be distracted by unproductive activities (usually because of their highly sociable nature).
	Summary: enthusiastic, curious, communicative and affiliative, but they need to be kept focused as they can lose interest.
6. THE MONITOR EVALUATOR • Particularly successful with skills of analysis: they focus on facts, analysing and evaluating ideas for their value, relevance and practicality • Builds on the suggestions of others – turning ideas into practical applications	• Successful Monitor Evaluators combine critical skills of analysis and evaluation with practical, results-oriented approach • They often possess strong leadership qualities, but can be undone by their too much scepticism and cynicism

195

Belbin's team preferences and their characteristics	Key points for leaders
• Provides clear thinking, offering firm and realistic arguments for rejecting unsound approaches • Balances innovation and experimentation with the practical needs of the task	Weaknesses: 1. Can be too negative with their critical skills outweighing their openness to new ideas. 2. They can be competitive with other team members. 3. The combination of 1 and 2 can lower morale! 4. In a non-directive team role they can find it hard not to appear threatening to other team members. Whereas in a directive role they can stifle contributions. **Summary: does things right and is careful, rational, methodical and analytical, but can over-emphasise detail and lack vision or inspiration.**
7. THE TEAM WORKER **Strong team workers that encourage and support others** • Promotes team spirit and effectiveness. Leads by example and is often selfless in their outlook • Has good interpersonal skills, improves team communications and develops relationships • Works hard • Understands the strengths and weaknesses of the team and acts accordingly	• Generally tough and determined, team workers persevere and have a strong sense of duty • They are conscientious and do not tend to ignore detail • Team workers can appear at any level in the team: from new recruit to team leader Weaknesses: 1. Loyalty to the team can override their focus on the task. 2. Tend to avoid resolving tough problems and conflict situations. **Summary: sensitive and a valuable team player with good interpersonal skills, but can be anxious and indecisive.**

Belbin's team preferences and their characteristics	Key points for leaders
8. THE COMPLETER FINISHER • Completer Finishers provide an all round perspective necessary for completing a task or project. They bring a focus on quality and an attention to detail, ensuring that tasks are completed as well as possible • They raise the standards of the team's activities • They inject urgency, priority and purpose into the team	• As a manager a Completer Finisher needs to avoid interfering and work on their delegation and empowerment skills. In a more junior role the CF can be perceived as a fussing worrier • They are hugely valuable in driving the team forward, achieving the task at a pace and to a standard that is as good as they can make it • They find mistakes in the detail, and they can identify aspects of the task that need more work Weaknesses: 1. Over-emphasising detail at the expense of the overall plan. 2. Lowering motivation and morale by worrying, perfectionism and undue criticism. <u>Summary</u>: **Conscientious, provides focus and has a strong ability to follow through, but has a tendency to worry and a reluctance to let go.**

Table 6 Belbin's team types

Key stages of team development

There are many different views concerning the evolution of successful teams, but most tend to follow the same pattern. The one that is used most frequently and perhaps most clearly defines the development of teams is the four stages of team development: *forming, storming, norming* and *performing*.

1. *Forming* – the team is a collection of individuals that are just starting to form into a single unit. The ice is carefully being broken, people are

197

introducing themselves and are generally quiet, polite and are getting the measure of others in the team.
2. *Storming* – conflict starts to emerge as people display their attitudes and set boundaries. This is an inevitable phase as people get to know others in the team and find their own identity.
3. *Norming* – norms are developed as people understand each other's strengths, weaknesses and patterns of behaviour. The group functions as a team and tasks are accomplished. Often teams settle at this level.
4. *Performing* – the team starts excelling and performing at its very best. This largely results from a steady accumulation of trust, respect and understanding, combined with a common sense of purpose and some successes.

To these four stages can be added a fifth – *reforming* – which refers to the process of renewing and reinvigorating the team, perhaps after failures, difficulties or major changes.

Team behaviour characteristics	*Leader's role to ensure team development*
Forming	
• Individuals make judgements of each other	• Gain team support for the vision, values and direction
• Individuals look to make friends and 'alliances'	• Build a supportive atmosphere
• The atmosphere is polite and co-operative	• Keep asserting the team's objectives
• The 'team' is little more than a group of individuals	• Get the team to start working together
	• Clarify roles, expectations and personal objectives to individuals
	• Enable relationships to form and give people time to find their role and strengths in the team
Storming	
• Attack the rules and structure that the team must operate within	• Keep asserting the vision, values processes and objectives
• Criticise the leader	• Renegotiate processes, procedures and structures within the team and with the rest of the organisation
• Criticise and challenge each other	
• Display sensitivity and act defensively	
• Unsurprisingly, low morale, motivation and confidence!	• Clarify (and enforce) the process for decision-making

TEAM-BUILDING AND DEVELOPING HIGH-PERFORMING TEAMS

Team behaviour characteristics	Leader's role to ensure team development
	• Limit personal attacks, defuse and resolve conflicts by identifying the *issues* • Move the team from 'testing and proving' to a problem-solving mentality • Stay positive, calm, cheerful and confident!
Norming • Consistent team behaviour begins to emerge • Ground-rules are accepted • The team focuses on its purpose and objectives • Mutual support begins, information is shared and team members co-operate effectively	• Prioritise objectives • Encourage development, provide feedback to the team and to individuals and encourage the team to provide feedback to each other • Show flexibility and promote openness • Encourage the team's input instead of telling • Confront problems and resolve issues with the team • Co-ordinate and facilitate the team's efforts – acting as a Chairperson • Represent the team to others (inside and outside the organisation)
Performing • The team is highly focused with a high degree of commitment • Team is functioning well: tasks are rapidly prioritised and assigned • Individual skills are continuing to improve and combine to achieve excellent results • The quality of the work accomplished exceeds expectations (in terms of standard and time taken)	• Provide feedback and encourage the team to openly provide feedback • Celebrate successes: this may mean telling others outside the team as well as rewarding the team performance • Be prepared to relinquish greater control to the team • Delegate, mentor and develop team members • Maintain momentum, set challenges and keep the team focused on new horizons

Team behaviour characteristics	Leader's role to ensure team development
Reforming • The team is becoming tired, disillusioned, losing momentum • Disagreements and criticisms emerge • Work rate falls both in terms of quality and quantity • The team is attacked and criticised from outside	• Find ways to renew, reintegrate and reinvigorate the team (i.e. consider new resources, new purpose) • Integrate the best of the past into the present • Provide a fresh vision and new challenges • If necessary, revert to an earlier phase of development

Table 7 Stages of team development

Techniques for effective team leading

Features of a good team leader

Good team leaders need to be able to:

- Gain the trust and commitment of their team members, relating to people as individuals.
- Mobilise and involve people in the team – getting the best from each person and motivating them.
- Recognise and unlock people's potential by *empowering* and *enabling*.
- Encourage people to solve problems.
- Provide opportunities to their team members.
- Provide support.
- Encourage people to innovate, experiment and take the initiative by fostering a positive, blame-free environment.
- Coach, facilitate and guide their team, often acting as a sounding board.
- Co-ordinate team efforts, both *within* the team and with others *outside* the team.
- Establish a reward system that satisfies the needs both of the team as well as individuals.
- Promote on the basis of merit.
- Encourage people who have the desire to excel and the ability to work constructively with others.
- Encourage questions and foster open discussion.
- Be proactive in their relationships.
- Inspire teamwork and mutual support.

TEAM-BUILDING AND DEVELOPING HIGH-PERFORMING TEAMS

- Stimulate action and excitement.
- Lead by example.
- Develop and clearly communicate a powerful vision, setting direction for their team.
- Show sensitivity, awareness and understanding, monitoring conflict and intervening before it becomes too destructive.
- Be able to give and receive feedback.
- Set goals with team members and discuss expectations.
- Understand how teams work, and develop their own style for forming, developing and leading them.

Features of a good team

- Individuals within the team recognise their mutual dependence on each other, and understand that this is the best way to achieve personal and team success (people do not waste time trying to achieve success at the expense of others).
- Team members work at understanding each other, and communicate honestly and openly.
- Members take a mature view of conflict, realising that it is unavoidable, trying to conflict as swiftly as possible, and looking to generate new ideas and understanding as a result.
- Team members feel a sense of pride and ownership in the team, and are committed to the team's success.
- Members trust and respect each other.
- Members encourage and support each other – sharing information and experience and communicating openly.
- Individuals understand when the leader needs to act and make a decision (i.e. in an emergency or if there is a major problem or disagreement).
- Team members are relaxed, determined and dynamic: they know the team and understand their own strengths and weaknesses.

Identifying and avoiding problems with teams

Problems developing in teams are often highlighted by the following behaviours:

- Uncharacteristic or prolonged dissent or unhappiness about the job, other team members or the leader.
- People work independently.
- People change their working routine – for example, increasing their out-of-hours working.
- Team members work at cross-purposes, undermining each other unintentionally or deliberately.

- Initiative and responsibility are lacking: people are told what to do or wait to be told what to do.
- People are wary of each other, perhaps even afraid to clearly speak their mind, motives are not trusted and the atmosphere is overly political.
- Domineering members of the team restrict contributions from others.
- Tensions and conflicts increase and can become harder to resolve quickly and amicably.
- Team members do not participate in decisions affecting the team: they withdraw from the group and no longer feel personal responsibility for success or failure.

Summary:	*Understanding team-building*
	Team-building is a continuing process requiring energy, commitment, feedback and review. Factors affecting the team change constantly, and the team needs to have the leadership and support that breeds flexibility and confidence. It is often useful to consider one's own career and reflect back to when you were in a successful team: what made it work and how could it have been better? Could your current team be improved?

Further information

Creating Top Flight Teams
H. Owen, Kogan Page, 1996

Management Teams: Why they succeed or fail
R.M. Belbin, William Heinemann, 1981

How to Lead a Winning Team
S. Morris, G. Willcocks, E. Knasel, FT/Pitman, 1995

High-performing Teams
M. Colenso, Butterworth-Heinemann, 1996

Build a Great Team
R. Jay, FT/Pitman, 1995

Time management

Introduction

Time management is critically important to the task of leadership for several reasons: first, poor time management can easily undermine the efficiency and authority of a leader, and often sets a poor example. Second, time management and the efficient prioritising and completion of tasks is one of the commonest areas for problems at work, and the leader needs to know *how* to manage time so that they can pass on the skills to colleagues. (For example, poor management of time is probably the single biggest factor causing stress at work.) Third, time management underpins so many other functions of leadership – such as delegating, motivating and team-building – that it is important for it to be completely mastered and understood to ensure effective leadership. This section therefore outlines techniques for managing time in order both to improve personal effectiveness and also to help others.

Peter Drucker and John Adair, two prominent leadership writers, have both acknowledged the view that *'only when we can manage time can we manage anything'*. Adair was one of the first management thinkers to emphasise the critical importance of time management and its central role in focusing action and helping leaders to achieve goals. For Adair, time management is not simply about being organised or efficient, or completing certain tasks: it is about managing time with a focus on achievement. Time management should be goal-driven and results-oriented and success in time management should be measured both by the *quantity* of work covered and the *quality* of both the work and the person's private life.

Checklist – time management techniques

1. Developing a personal sense of time

Time management is an entirely personal activity, yet quite often individuals will expect their time to be managed by others and they will assume that their manager understands their priorities and workload. The starting place for efficient time management is the fundamental principle that each person – at any level in the organisation – needs to develop a personal sense of time. This means:

- Taking responsibility for managing your own time, setting goals and priorities.
- Using all of your time to the greatest effect and planning your use of time.
- Taking action to ensure that manageable pressure does not become intolerable stress because of problems with time. If it does, then you will need to take action to remedy the situation.

2. Planning your use of time

Frequently people rush at their work without planning: they either believe that they do not have the time to plan, or they think that even if they do it won't make a difference. To succeed, planning needs to be done regularly and routinely, and its value needs to be clearly understood. It is not just about listing tasks, but about analysing and prioritising them too. There are three levels of planning:

- *Identifying long-term goals* – this means understanding what you want to achieve in the next year and beyond; where your career is going, what goals you want to complete and perhaps most importantly what skills you need to develop during this period. (For instance, many people write down long-term goals at the start of each year.)
- *Making medium-term plans* – these can cover anything from the next few days to the next three months: it really does depend on the environment and situation that you are in. For instance, in some industries a few days may be critical and require detailed planning, whereas for most people a longer time frame is helpful to set goals and priorities.
- *Planning the day* – it is remarkably easy for time to pass on unproductive tasks, and the best approach is to decide what needs to be accomplished that day, how long it will need and when the task will start and finish. It is worth analysing each task and asking:

    1. Is it really necessary?
    2. Is it better done (or more appropriately done) by someone else?
    3. Can it reasonably be delegated?
    4. What is the appropriate quality standard required for this work?
    5. How urgent is it relative to the other tasks for today? One technique here is to prioritise work on a scale of A–C, where A is the most important task(s); B tasks are important but not as important as A, and C tasks are those that are desirable to complete but can wait if necessary.

Also, it may only be a part of the project rather than the whole that can be completed (for example, in writing this book I have set aside two hours each day), but it is still important in making progress. The daily plan, therefore, needs to link with the medium-term one, and they both need to recognise the need to move in the direction of the long-term goals.

3. Organising and efficiently managing your work

Using committed time, such as travelling, is important, together with identifying and removing time-stealers such as unnecessary meetings. Key elements of best practice include:

- organising office work;
- managing meetings (e.g. having an agenda and clear purpose; keeping comments and contributions relevant and focused, and following up with an agreed list of action points);
- delegating effectively.

4. Using skills of assertion

Time pressures can frequently result from people being 'put upon' or asked to do tasks that they feel they cannot refuse. The antidote to this is assertion and includes:

- Communicating your feelings and priorities clearly, firmly and politely.
- Understanding that you can say no – or not at the moment.
- Not being afraid of silence – often people feel obliged to fill an expectant pause by volunteering. If you are obliged to say something then briefly explain why it cannot be you this time.
- Getting the ground-rules right with employees, suppliers, customers and colleagues. For example, avoid getting into a routine where you are expected to be the one that takes on the extra work.
- Ensuring that the job description is fair and appropriate, and taking steps to change it if necessary.
- Not being afraid to ask for help when you need it.

5. Managing your health

Looking after yourself is a vital – and frequently neglected – aspect of time management. This does not only mean managing time pressures so as to reduce and handle the causes of stress; it also means ensuring that even when you are not under stress you are in the best physical condition possible. This will then enable you to focus on work, completing tasks efficiently and as soon as possible. Managing your health may therefore involve remedying any ills quickly rather than letting them drag on and debilitate; eating a balanced diet and taking reasonable exercise. If these are difficult to achieve then at least understand the state in which you function best and try to preserve this.

> **Summary:** *Identifying time-based problems*
>
> As a leader it is important that you are aware of people's techniques for managing time, and guide them as to the best approach for themselves, their team and the organisation as a whole. Some of the time-related problems that leaders may notice and need to resolve in others include:
>
> - *Laziness and poor time-keeping* – does the person simply need to improve their time-keeping, arriving and leaving on time and not gossiping too much with others, for example?
> - *Work avoidance* – often people will avoid difficult or unpleasant tasks or 'lurkers' (so called because they lurk in the bottom of the in-tray!). These tasks need to be hit hard and early before they can fester and grow …
> - *Passing the buck* – does the person use their assertiveness skills too much, routinely passing on work that they should complete themselves? This can often generate time management problems, as well as resentment and 'people problems' elsewhere in the organisation. (I once worked in a team where the manager left for an extended holiday, and the question that swept the office was 'Who will do David's work while he is away?' Answer: 'The same people that do it when he's here!')
> - *Under-employment* – if someone does not have enough work to do, that too may cause problems (from disrupting others to tinkering needlessly and causing additional work).
> - *Disruptive conditions* – is the team able to focus and work productively, or are there constant disruptions and distractions that both reduces the quality of work *and* increases the quantity that needs to be done?

- *Stress resulting from time management difficulties* – the symptoms and causes of stress were outlined in a previous section, and a contributory factor in many instances of stress is time pressures, including deadlines and volume of work that needs to be completed.

Clearly the leader needs to be aware of these difficulties at the very least: identifying time-based problems and resolving them, if only by speaking to the people involved.

Further information

First Things First
P. Forsyth, FT/Pitman, 1994

Successfully Managing Time in a Week
D. Treacy, Hodder Headline, 1993

Personal Effectiveness
A. Murdock and C. Scutt, Butterworth-Heinemann, 1993

Time is Money: Save it
L. Seiwert, Kogan Page, 1991

Total quality management (TQM) and business process re-engineering (BPR)

Introduction

Total quality management (TQM) is the process of ensuring that goods or services meet the customers' needs and wants. Total commitment and involvement at all levels of the organisation are essential for this to be achieved, but the process also requires *leadership* to be successful. The characteristics of TQM include:

- Meeting the customers' needs.
- Consistently maintaining a minimum quality standard for products and services.
- Ensuring that goods and services are delivered on time.
- Providing after-sales service that maintains and develops customer confidence.

There are a number of approaches to quality management generally the following features are regarded as being essential prerequisites:

- Quality is a responsibility of the organisation's *leadership,* who set, implement and monitor quality targets.
- Quality is also a responsibility of all *employees* whose work needs to meet the quality targets.
- Quality is an attitude and an integral part of the organisation's culture: it runs through everything that the organisation does (instilling the right attitude is therefore an essential starting point – but it clearly takes time to achieve).
- Quality needs to be constantly monitored and developed to keep pace with customer's needs and expectations. It is therefore a dynamic, continuous process rather than a static goal.

Key principles of total quality management

Quality management techniques have historically been applied to the manufacturing industry, and many of the techniques and momentum for TQM originated from the approach of Japanese industry to mass production. However, manufacturing is now seen as being only one part of the whole process of satisfying customer needs. Quality is therefore relevant to *all* parts of the organisation's operations.

For organisations to pursue a total quality management policy successfully the following points are essential:

Management commitment

As with any organisation-wide initiative the leadership and senior management must show constant, visible support to the principles of TQM. This commitment needs to cascade the principles of TQM throughout the organisation.

Quality policy

The leadership of the organisation needs to develop a quality policy that is clearly understood and applied as widely as possible. The goal of the policy is to emphasise the importance of quality throughout the business and to change attitudes: in this sense it needs to have a strategic tone rather than being an operational procedures manual.

Instilling a quality culture

The procedural aspects of TQM are important, but they are nothing without the commitment of *everyone* in the organisation, regardless of their position. This is because quality cannot simply be inspected in or added on to a product or service – if this happens inevitably there will be faults that pass through this process. Instead it needs to be built in at the planning stage.

Continuous improvement

A second reason for ensuring that everyone within the organisation embraces total quality and accepts responsibility for the quality of the product or service supplied is the concept of *continuous improvement*. If quality means meeting and exceeding customer needs then it is clearly not a static process, but one requiring change and improvement. The only way to obtain this is with the support of the people operating the processes: they are the ones best placed to identify problems and suggest practical solutions. Improvements do not need to be quantum leaps: small, incremental improvements are often more manageable to implement and keep the organisation moving forward steadily, rather than lurching which can cause stresses in a number of areas.

People management aspects of TQM

Clearly people need to be motivated for TQM to work. Explaining the rationale helps, so does:

- Showing commitment and leading by example.
- Finding areas where change can be initiated.
- Achieving early successes.
- Getting the support of key individuals and teams.
- Incorporating TQM into the strategy, team and individual objectives.
- Team working and communicating between teams and departments. It is vital to ensure that one area's quality improvement does not become someone else's latest problem!
- Training people to implement TQM. This is often the largest aspect of the TQM budget as staff require training in: the purpose and philosophy of TQM; quality management techniques; how to use quality systems, and team working.
- Motivating people with reward systems such as performance-related bonuses.

Quality techniques

There is a wide range of techniques and tools for managing quality, and some of the most popular include:

- *Quality circles* – these involve a broad range of employees, from all levels in the organisation, in finding new ways to improve quality. The emphasis is on regular meetings led by a facilitator: brainstorming is one technique used to develop creative and alternative approaches. Quality circles originated – and remain – a powerful feature of Japanese manufacturing industry.
- *Quality audit* – this is similar to its financial counterpart in that it involves an investigation by specialists seeking out defects and potential problem areas.
- *Quality costing* – it is possible to assess the cost of quality for an organisation. This cost includes:
  - *Failure costs* – the result of having to rework substandard products or provide additional service due to poor performance.
  - *Preventative costs* – the cost of putting procedures in place to prevent failure.
  - *Appraisal costs* – the cost of testing products to ensure that they meet the quality standard specified.

ONE STOP LEADERSHIP

- *Opportunity cost* is another factor resulting from poor or inconsistent quality. The cost of improvement needs to be carefully monitored and measured against the costs of not making the improvement.
- *Statistical process control (SPC)* – this technique is used for monitoring the quality of output from a process or machine so that any problems can be identified and corrected as quickly as possible.

The quality spiral effect

Quality improvements can become a self-sustaining process with the following stages:

- clearly defining the standards that are required;
- collecting full information on current performance, and deciding what changes are needed to match achievements with goals;
- implementing the necessary changes;
- monitoring and evaluating the effects of the changes.

These stages combine as follows:

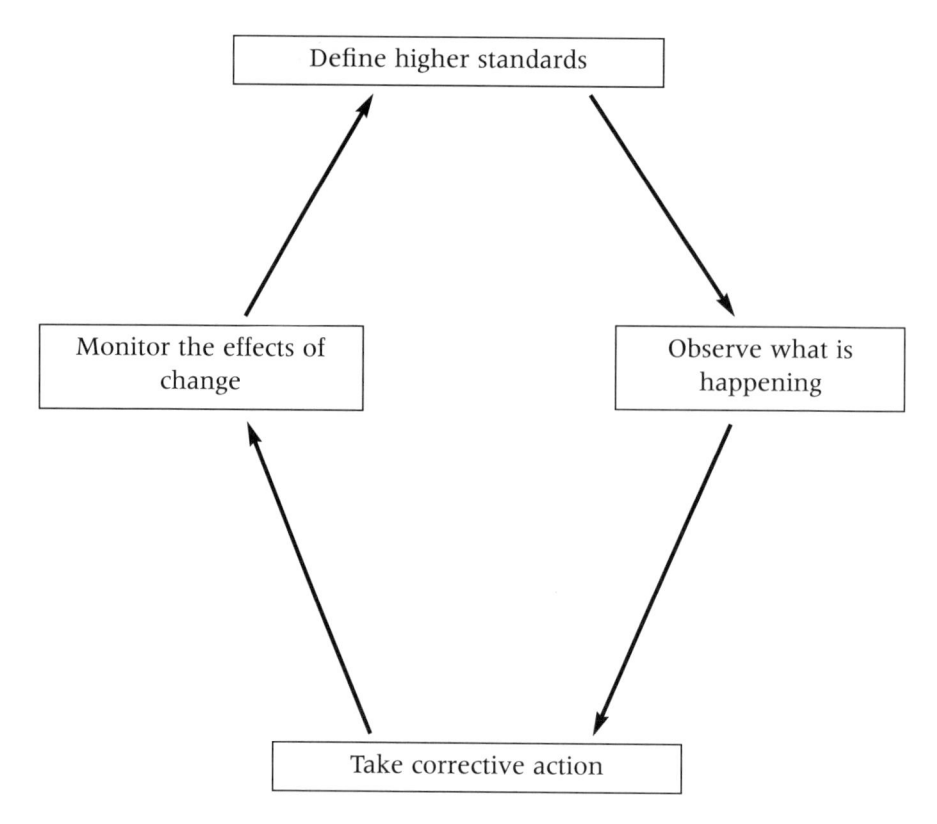

Figure 2 Stages of quality improvement

The cumulative effect of each of these changes is a steady, consistent improvement in quality and sustained momentum for change.

Business process re-engineering (BPR)

BPR is a term used to cover three separate approaches to managing change:

1. Process improvement

This approach includes TQM as well as other techniques such as Kaizen, and generally emphasises steady, continuous improvement in every aspect of the organisation's activities. These improvements tend to be small but taken together move the organisation steadily in the desired direction.

2. Process redesign

This is a natural evolution of TQM and it uses many of the same techniques, but it is much more concerned with significant change rather than improvement. It concentrates on the major processes that cross functional boundaries and constantly asks *'should we be doing this process at all?'*

3. Process re-engineering

This takes the view that steady, incremental improvements can be quite inadequate to satisfy the needs of some organisations, due to the pace of change, globalisation, increasing use of technology and a number of other factors that organisations (mostly commercial) face. Doing the same process another way (process redesign) is also quite inadequate. The process re-engineering approach relies on radical, dramatic change to achieve major breakthroughs in performance, i.e. cutting cost by 50 per cent whilst at the same time improving quality and shortening lead-times; or cutting development and production cycles by 40 per cent in order to beat competitors.

If TQM is continuous improvement, then process re-engineering can be thought of as discontinuous improvement. Michael Hammer defines re-engineering as:

> *a fundamental rethink and radical redesign of business processes to achieve dramatic improvements in critical contemporary measures of performance, such as cost, quality, speed and service.*

How re-engineering works

John Macdonald, one of the UK's foremost experts on implementing BPR and performance improvements, outlines four phases for successfully completing a re-engineering process. The process as a whole can last for over two years and follows a clear sequence:

Phase 1 – Preparation

- defining objectives
- training and developing the team
- mapping the overall process model (including sub-processes)
- defining customer needs
- defining the strategic needs of the business
- outlining potential breakthroughs and areas on which to focus
- preparing objectives
- obtaining approval to proceed.

Phase 2 – Innovation and design

- visioning and encouraging innovation
- using IT
- ensuring realism and the practical application of innovations
- cost-benefit analysis
- preparing the organisation for change
- planning implementation.

Phase 3 – Implementation

- piloting proposed changes to ensure they are fully effective and work as expected
- setting goals and objectives, particularly in terms of cost, quality and timescale, for the implementation process
- training, motivating and mobilising people to achieve the desired goals
- using multidisciplinary teams to gather together the necessary range of skills
- ensuring effective communication.

Phase 4 – Assessment

This part of the process is concerned with making any adjustments and continuous improvements, and it also emphasises the vital importance of *consolidation* – holding the gains so that they become embedded in the organisation.

- recognising the change
- managing the re-engineered business – ensuring that new systems and structures are in place where necessary
- managing people, i.e. meeting concerns and maintaining team work and motivation
- maintaining and exploiting the gains.

Summary: *Total quality management*

The philosophy of total quality management is summed up in the phrase 'right first time', and it is an overall approach to meeting customers' needs. In general, TQM can only be introduced to an organisation once: if it succeeds it will become part of the culture, but if it fails there is usually such cynicism and resentment that it cannot then be raised again. There are two elements to the quality task:

1. *Task* – successfully developing staff awareness and attitudes to quality; establishing methods for consistent quality control, and creating effective channels for improving quality.
2. *Response* – implementing an overall programme for training and developing staff in quality management techniques; regular quality audits, and quality circles to identify methods for continuous improvement.

Key aspects of TQM

- TQM involves culture change and needs time to take effect *in any size of organisation.*
- The process needs to be supported and 'driven' from the top of the organisation down.
- TQM involves everyone in the organisation, at all levels.
- Customers are the focus for TQM, both internally (i.e. other departments) as well as externally.
- Reducing waste and costs are also fundamental to TQM – and the whole process is about looking for ways of improving service to customers and efficiency *whilst simultaneously* cutting costs.
- To achieve this, systems and procedures must be continuously improved and staff often need training in the necessary skills and approach to ensure that this happens.

Further information

Total Quality Management
J. Oakland, Butterworth-Heinemann, 1989

Calling a Halt to Mindless Change
J. Macdonald, McGraw-Hill, 1998

Successful Business Process Re-engineering in a Week
J. Macdonald, Hodder Headline, 1995

Managing Quality for the First Time
D. Cranswick, FT/Pitman, 1996

Vision and transformation

> **Introduction**
>
> A real test of a leader's skill is their ability to create and communicate an effective vision for their organisation or team. This is what often defines a successful leader and sustains both the leader and the team/organisation during good times and bad. One of the reasons that leaders come to the fore is because people generally need to know where they are going, and what the overall purpose of their activity is: one of the reasons, therefore, that people need a leader is because they want a positive vision of the future.
>
> Developing a successful vision often means changing – or transforming – the organisation so that it can move in a determined way in the right direction. Vision and transformation are therefore closely interrelated in the same process of leadership.

Visioning

John Kotter in his hugely popular and influential book *Leading Change* identified a number of elements of a successful vision. In brief, a successful vision must be:

- *Realistic* – it must comprise feasible, attainable goals.
- *Powerful* – this has two parts: it must be *imaginable* and paint a clear picture of what the future will look like; it must also *excite and inspire* as many people as possible.
- *Communicable* – it must be possible for the vision to be communicated to anyone, *quickly* (within a few minutes) and *easily* (without burying them in pie charts, reports, projections…).
- *Desirable* – the vision needs to appeal to the long-term interests of all the stakeholders; for a business these may chiefly include customers, employees, shareholders.
- *Focused* – the vision needs to be specific and 'real-world' enough to be used as a basis for strategic planning, and to provide guidance for decision-making.
- *Adaptive* – the vision needs to be general enough to allow individual

initiative in how it is attained, and flexible enough to allow for changing conditions.

The process of developing and successfully realising a vision has several key elements:

1. developing the vision
2. actively communicating the vision at all levels
3. using – or implementing – the vision
4. coping with problems and difficulties
5. learning and adapting.

> **Case study:** *'I have a dream'*
>
> The history of politics is covered with sparkling examples of powerful visions that have inspired large numbers of people to great achievements. Martin Luther King's rallying call to Americans contained in his dramatic 'I have a dream' speech is one powerful example. President Kennedy's inaugural address in which he urged his countrymen to 'ask not what your country can do for you, ask what you can do for your country', is another example. So was Nelson Mandela's defence speech at his trial in the early 1960s.
>
> I believe that the reason these speeches (or visions) – and others – are so successful is because:
>
> 1. They tap into the needs of the audience, who positively *want* to be led and inspired.
> 2. They are clear, simple and unequivocal. They don't ask, they tell.
> 3. They generate confidence, not just in what is said but how and who is saying it. This means that the vision must be credible – and that means coming from the right person at the right time.
> 4. They appeal to characteristics that are universally popular: determination, integrity, success, fairness, etc.
>
> Winston Churchill made a career of capturing the moment with powerful, visionary speeches, and I am sure everyone has a favourite speech or quotation.

VISION AND TRANSFORMATION

GOAL:	TECHNIQUES:
DEVELOPING THE VISION How this is achieved depends on the style of the leader, and may range from a consensus approach to a more directive style.	• For a commercial organisation, consider the major changes in your markets alongside developments in technology and competitor activity. What would be the most effective, flexible and profitable direction to take? • Decide which factors matter most: long-term success; short-term survival; adapting the organisation to coming changes; transforming the organisation to be more profitable/customer-focused/pioneering/risk-averse etc. • Cascading the need for a clear vision to other senior managers so that they can contribute to the process from the perspective of their own job function. • Finally, look ahead to the vision that you have developed and assume that you have achieved it by bringing about the necessary transformation. What would you be most satisfied with about that transformation?
ACTIVELY COMMUNICATING THE VISION AT ALL LEVELS For the vision to have greatest value it needs to be shared and accepted, and whilst this may not be essential it is certainly desirable. Achieving agreement and unity around a common purpose is therefore a valuable aspect of leadership and will make progress to achieving the vision swifter and more likely.	• Using powerful and emotive language and images to describe the vision, mobilising and enervating people. • Explain what is needed from people and what factors should guide their actions (ideally in priority order). • When explaining, take care to avoid patronising and over-simplifying, or the opposite and assuming too much knowledge.

GOAL:	TECHNIQUES:
USING THE VISION To be fully effective the vision needs to routinely guide actions and plans across the organisation and at all levels.	• Leading by example will demonstrate how the vision will influence your decisions and actions. • The leader needs to gain momentum and support for the vision with examples and early successes. • Steadily reinforcing the vision with examples of successes and news of initiatives will help to develop its constant use. • Getting the understanding and commitment of key managers and influencers (e.g. unions) will also help in the practical application of the vision.
COPING WITH PROBLEMS OR DIFFICULTIES Clearly the vision needs to be flexible and able to cope with changing circumstances. Given that the only constant is change the vision will be fatally flawed and doomed to failure if it is too rigid or inflexible.	In developing the vision it is worth asking yourself: • What are the weaknesses with this approach? • What are others doing, and how is the situation likely to alter over time? • Are the people involved prepared (in terms of attitude) and skilled (in terms of ability) to react to changing situations? How can this be measured? What remedial action might be needed? • What is likely to prevent you and your colleagues from fulfilling your vision? • How will you and your colleagues pre-empt these challenges, or react to any unforeseen problems?

VISION AND TRANSFORMATION

GOAL:	TECHNIQUES:
LEARNING AND ADAPTING The leader needs to ensure that the organisation is fully prepared for the process of transformation and achieving the vision. This means not only developing people's skills, but developing their attitudes and approaches as well. What matters is not simply what people know, *but how they react to what they do not know.*	• Commitment is a fundamental prerequisite for learning and preparing to meet the challenges ahead – the leader needs to generate the necessary pressure and commitment. • Learning and professional development is a constant, continuous process. Consider how this culture of constant personal development can be actively encouraged and fostered.

Table 8 Key elements of visionary leadership

Summary: *Strategic advantages of visionary leadership*

It is worth considering the strategic advantages of visionary leadership.

1. *It builds self-confidence.* A clear vision of the future and where the business is heading gives leaders the confidence to take action that has long-term consequences.
2. *It inspires.* Visionary leadership can be highly motivating – it quickly builds respect, motivating and enthusing people to act.
3. *It provides a sense of direction.* This may seem obvious but it is none the less an important part of motivating people to succeed. This aspect of vision is particularly valuable in uncharted situations where people have little or no experience.
4. *It can provide timely innovation, anticipating new opportunities.* The ability to visualise new situations – creating a vision of the future – is often the key to achieving 'first-mover advantage' and exploiting major new opportunities.
5. *It ensures that communication is powerful and effective.* A clear vision is an important aid in getting the

> message across, and it can be useful in influencing people and focusing people's actions.
>
> Vision and strategy are complex, interwoven topics, but the key to ensuring success in these matters – as with many others – is developing a personal style of leadership that can develop and sustain success.

Further information

The Fish Rots from the Head
B. Garratt, HarperCollins, 1996

A Sense of Mission
M. Campbell, M. Devine, David Young, Hutchinson, 1990

Built to Last: Successful habits of visionary companies
J. Collins and G. Porras, HarperCollins, 1994